Easy PC Care

D1379486

Teach® Yourself

Easy PC Care

Anthony Price

For UK order enquiries: please contact Bookpoint Ltd,
130 Milton Park, Abingdon, Oxon OX14 4SB.
Telephone: +44 (0) 1235 827720. Fax: +44 (0) 1235 400454.
Lines are open 09.00–17.00, Monday to Saturday, with a 24-hour
message answering service. Details about our titles and how to
order are available at www.teachyourself.com

Long renowned as the authoritative source for self-guided
learning – with more than 50 million copies sold worldwide –
the **Teach Yourself** series includes over 500 titles in the fields of
languages, crafts, hobbies, business, computing and education.

British Library Cataloguing in Publication Data: a catalogue record
for this title is available from the British Library.

First published in UK 2010 by Hodder Education, part of
Hachette UK, 338 Euston Road, London NW1 3BH.

The **Teach Yourself** name is a registered trade mark of
Hodder Headline.

Typeset by MPS Limited, A Macmillan Company.

Printed in Great Britain for Hodder Education, an Hachette UK
Company, 338 Euston Road, London NW1 3BH, by CPI Cox &
Wyman, Reading, Berkshire RG1 8EX.

The publisher has used its best endeavours to ensure that the URLs
for external websites referred to in this book are correct and active
at the time of going to press. However, the publisher and the
author have no responsibility for the websites and can make no
guarantee that a site will remain live or that the content will remain
relevant, decent or appropriate.

Hachette UK's policy is to use papers that are natural, renewable
and recyclable products and made from wood grown in sustainable
forests. The logging and manufacturing processes are expected to
conform to the environmental regulations of the country of origin.

Impression number   10 9 8 7 6 5 4 3 2 1
Year   2014 2013 2012 2011 2010

Contents

Welcome to easy PC Care   ix
Only got a minute?   xii
Only got five minutes?   xiv
Only got ten minutes?   xx

1 Maintaining Windows   1
    Windows versions   1
    Four things you can do now   2
    The Disk Cleanup Wizard   4
    The Disk Defragmenter   6
    Visual Effects   8
    Using Safe Mode   9
    Using the Repair your Computer option   11

2 Backups and system images   14
    Backups   16
    System images   19
    System Restore   24
    Shadow copies   31

3 Control Panel   34
    System and Security   39
    User Accounts and Family Safety   44
    Network and Internet   46
    Appearance and Personalization   47
    Hardware and Sound   50
    Clock, language and region   53
    Programs   54
    Ease of access   54

4 Making a support call   56
    Before you call for Help   56
    Defining the problem   57
    Gathering the information   58
    Calling the Help Desk   62
    Finding a PC technician   62

5	**The command line prompt**	**67**
	Why use a command prompt?	67
	Accessing a command line prompt	68
	Command syntax	69
	The command set	71
	Batch files and CMD scripts	75
6	**Backup strategies**	**79**
	Backups	79
	Backup types	83
	CMOS/BIOS settings	86
7	**Inside the box**	**90**
	Working safely	90
	The main components	92
	Why some things aren't worth upgrading	99
8	**Replacing and upgrading hardware**	**102**
	Before you start	102
	How to add RAM modules	103
	Replacing a power supply unit	106
	How to add a second hard disk	108
	How to add or replace a CD or DVD drive	114
	How to fit a floppy drive	115
	How to fit a PCI expansion card	118
	How to fit a PCI-e or AGP graphics card	119
	How to replace a motherboard	120
9	**Preventive maintenance**	**124**
	A maintenance schedule	124
	Cleaning products and tools	126
	Cleaning	127
	Safety	131
10	**Peripheral devices**	**134**
	Ports	134
	Device drivers	143
11	**Printers**	**147**
	Common printer types	148
	Printer connection methods	152
	Installing a printer	153
	Sharing a printer on a network	156

Obtaining drivers and manuals   158
What to do if your printer doesn't work   160
12 Components and programs   **163**
Installing programs   168
Turn Windows features on or off   173
Default programs   173
13 Installing/reinstalling Windows   **179**
How to avoid a reinstall   179
How to prepare for a reinstall   181
Windows Easy Transfer   184
An OEM install   188
A conventional install   189
Installing Windows 7   190
Post-install   199
14 Troubleshooting   **204**
The Troubleshooting wizards   204
Using Device Manager   206
Isolating the symptom   210
Separating software from hardware   211
Investigating the problem   212
Diagnostic utilities   214
Third-party tools   217
Some common problems and their solutions   219
15 The internet and e-mail   **221**
How to set up your Internet connection   221
Setting up a dialup connection   223
Installing a USB broadband modem   227
Installing a broadband modem/router   230
How to configure your web browser   235
How firewalls work   236
How e-mail works   239
16 Viruses and other malware   **242**
Viruses, trojans and worms   242
Basic precautions   243
Scheduling updates and scans   247
Windows Defender   249
SmartScreen Filter in Internet Explorer 8   250

InPrivate browsing   252
Parental control software   252
How to deal with a virus infection   253

17 Home networking   **257**
Networking with Windows 7   257
Hardware   257
Setting up the HomeGroup   259
Streaming media   269
Cloud storage   272

18 Wireless networking   **277**
Wireless Networking Standards   277
Ad-hoc wireless networks   280
Using an ad-hoc connection   284
Wireless access points   284
Wireless security   288
Other security measures   291
Index   **294**

Welcome to easy PC Care

This book grew out of several years of working as a PC support technician and as an Adult Education teacher of trainee technicians. It doesn't attempt to document every possible problem or to document every feature of a modern PC; at ten times the length it couldn't achieve that. Its aim is to give you a guided tour of a typical PC in terms of hardware basics and some of the technical tools provided with the Windows 7 operating system. For simple jobs I hope it will provide a handy reference; for more complex topics it provides an introduction, a point of departure for your own enquiries. I have assumed that you are familiar with the basics of Windows, that you can navigate through the menu system, point and click, and maybe even launch a command prompt. If you need to bring yourself up to speed with Windows 7, *Teach Yourself Getting Started in Windows 7* will provide a good primer.

This book is about the basics: the jobs you can do yourself on your PC with a bit of know-how and a screwdriver. If you can use a computer as an everyday tool for word processing, e-mail, etc. there are many jobs that you can handle. With the aid of *Teach Yourself Easy PC Care*, you can:

Maintain the system at peak efficiency
Manage anti-virus and security measures
Upgrade or add hard disks, CD and DVD drives or RAM
Replace a dead power supply unit
Diagnose software and hardware faults
Attach peripheral devices, e.g. a printer, scanner or
    camera, to the standard external ports
Set up and manage a home network to share an Internet
    connection and/or a printer or scanner.

Even where you decide that a job is too big for you – and you'll be surprised at what you can do for yourself if you're willing to have a go – you will be able to:

Make a support phone call clearly and with confidence
Discuss problems with a professional technical support
   worker in the language that they understand
Be sure that work proposed for your system is necessary
Check that all work is carried out effectively.

Teach Yourself Easy PC Care is not intended to turn you into a qualified PC technician: there are other books and courses which aim to do that. What it will do is save you money on your PC maintenance bills by putting you in control of your system. You will find that most PC maintenance is easy enough (when you know how) and once you have done a few jobs for yourself you may even find that you enjoy it!

Anthony Price

Only got a minute?

If you can change a light bulb, mend a fuse, or check the oil in your car you can do most of the things necessary to keep your PC working and working well.

Windows

Modern operating systems – like Windows 7 – provide graphical tools for maintaining the system and diagnosing faults. The examples in this book were tested on a system running Windows 7 Home Premium Edition. This is the most widely used Windows version for home users. Earlier versions of Windows such as Vista or XP provide much the same functionality and most of the things in this book will work on those earlier systems.

Hardware

To work with hardware all you need is a Phillips #2 screwdriver – though a few other tools may be useful – and the ability to follow step-by-step instructions. Modern hardware is generally robust and reliable, but if you *do* have to replace or upgrade anything (like a hard disk drive, say) it's usually a case of physically attaching the new component to the system and connecting power and data cables before powering up the PC and allowing the system to Plug and Play the new component.

Networking

Windows 7 makes home networking – wired or wireless – as intuitive as using a standalone PC. You can share files, printers, and Internet access between several users; you can synchronize your laptop with your family PC; you can drag and drop files and folders between PCs on your network; and all done without the need for technical knowledge.

5 Only got five minutes?

This book is written in terms of Windows 7 Home Premium Edition. This is the most popular version of the latest Windows release. Although it has a '7' in its brand name it is, in fact, Windows 6.1. To check this for yourself:

1 Click on the Start button.
2 Type 'CMD' in the Search box and press [Enter].

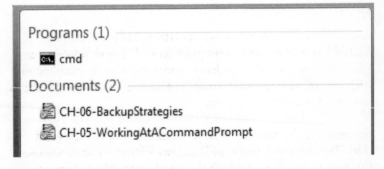

Programs (1)
■ cmd
Documents (2)
CH-06-BackupStrategies
CH-05-WorkingAtACommandPrompt

The search utility will list several items containing the text 'CMD'. The first item in the list is the CMD icon.

3 Click on the CMD icon.

This will start an instance of the Command line processor. You can see from the first line that Windows 7 is in fact Windows 6.1.

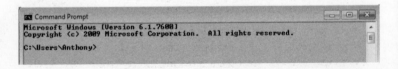

Command Prompt
Microsoft Windows [Version 6.1.7600]
Copyright (c) 2009 Microsoft Corporation. All rights reserved.

C:\Users\Anthony>

4 Close the CMD window.

Notice that Windows has added the launcher for CMD to your Start menu. If you right-click on the icon you will see a context menu that presents you with several choices:

Open
Run as administrator

Pin to Taskbar
Pin to Start Menu

Remove from this list

Properties

Most of these choices are self-explanatory. They will also be available as options for any program icon. The option to **Run as Administrator** is something that you may need when installing new programs where you wish to make the new application available to all users on a multi-user system.

The news that Windows 7 is really version 6.1 is, in fact, good news. The previous version of Windows – Vista – was version 6.0. This means that there is a high degree of compatibility between the two versions and that most topics presented in this book will – give or take a few details – work equally well in Vista. If you are still using Windows XP (Windows 5.x) a lot of the material presented will be useful, though you may find that utilities have a different appearance or may be accessed by different routes.

If you want to see an entirely different operating system you may find it interesting to try a 'live CD' version of one of the major Linux distributions such as Ubuntu or Linux Mint. Disk images can be downloaded from the Internet and are frequently found on PC magazine covers. You can boot your PC to the 'live CD' and see a working alternative to Windows without changing anything on your Windows system.

Hardware

Modern hardware is generally robust and reliable though you may occasionally need to replace or upgrade a component or two. As often as not you will be simply replacing like with like so all you need to do is to remove the old component and replace it with a new one. In terms of safety, you are more likely to damage a component than a component is likely to damage you. Apart from the power supply unit (PSU) the internal components of your PC work on 12 volts (DC) or less so the work hazard that you face when working with hardware is the odd scratch from occasional sharp edges on the case or a minor burn from touching hot internal components such as the CPU or disk drive.

To avoid damaging components:

1 Keep new components in the manufacturer's packaging until you are ready to use them.
2 Always power down the PC before opening the case.
3 Always touch a bare metal part of the case to discharge any static electricity in your body before handling any components (an anti-static wrist strap is better).

After you have fitted the new component, make sure that everything is properly seated and connected and that you have left no loose screws inside the case.

When you are sure that the new part is fitted correctly reboot the machine and see if Windows recognizes it. More often that not Windows 7 will recognize the new component and provide the necessary drivers to make it work 'out of the box'. Alternatively, you may have a manufacturer's CD containing drivers for the new device or you may decide to download the latest versions from the Internet. Either way, you will usually only have to point and click with a mouse and follow on-screen installation instructions. Peripheral devices such as printers, modems, etc. require a more or less similar approach.

Working with internal hardware is described in more detail in Chapters 7 and 8; peripheral ports and printers are the subjects of Chapters 10 and 11.

Networking

Home networking is an area that has really taken off in recent years and Widows 7 in particular makes home networking a straightforward point-and-click exercise. Obviously the PCs in question need to by physically connected either by Ethernet cables or wireless connections before you can set up your network. If you are using cables to connect you will need to plug them into to the RJ45 connectors on the backs of PCs that you are networking. If you are connecting two systems back to back you will need to use a crossover cable (a special network cable that has send and receive lines crossed over) or if you are connecting to a Workgroup Ethernet switch or ADSL switch/router you will need to use straight-through cables.

Windows 7 implements home networking through 'HomeGroup'. If you type 'homegroup' into the search box on the main menu you will see something like this:

Control Panel (4)

- HomeGroup
- Find and fix problems with homegroup
- Choose homegroup and sharing options
- Share printers

At this introductory stage it may be useful for you to explore the options available. We will return to networking more fully in Chapters 17 and 18.

Windows 7 uses a system called 'Network Discovery'. This system is turned on to be the default when Windows 7 is installed and is so effective that it practically sets up your home network for you automatically. There are, however, some restrictions. Any Windows 7 computer can join a HomeGroup and all versions except 'Starter' and 'Basic' can create one. Older Windows versions such as Vista and XP can also be connected to the HomeGroup, but will need a tweak or two to achieve this. This is covered later in the networking chapters.

To look at your HomeGroup status:

1 Type network into the search box on the **Start** menu.
2 Click on the Network and Sharing Center option.
3 Click on the See Full Map link (top right of the page) and you will see something like this:

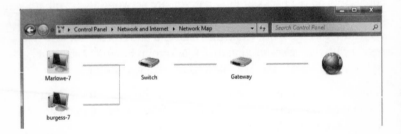

This figure shows a typical home network set-up. Two PCs – Marlowe-7 and Burgess-7 – are both connected to an Ethernet switch and, through this switch, to each other. The switch is in turn connected to a Gateway (or router) which gives both PCs access to the Internet.

Although the switch/router pair are shown as separate units they are in fact logical parts of a single ADSL modem/router that you can buy from an ordinary PC shop on the High Street.

If you want to explore further, the **Choose HomeGroup and Sharing** options link will show you the default settings for your workgroup. The associated Help system is also comprehensive and clear.

You will have seen the effectiveness of the Search box in Windows 7. This isn't a new technology, but its implementation is far more sophisticated and powerful than in earlier Windows versions. The Control Panel has its own search box which allows you to confine your search to the Control Panel rather than the system as a whole. Try it.

10 Only got ten minutes?

This is a book about doing things. You need not read or work through it in any particular order but before you start it is generally a good idea to get to know the system that you are working with, so we'll spend our ten minutes doing that.

If your system was built by one of the major manufacturers – Dell, e-machines, Sony, or their like – you will probably have documentation and software disks that were sold with your PC. These are a useful first source of information.

The Internet

In addition to documentation provided by manufacturers there is a mass of information available on the Internet which can be found by carrying out a search on the manufacturer's name and model number. If, for example, you search on ET1831-01 you will find that this is an e-machines model and in the first couple of pages of results you will find links to the manufacturer's site and the sites of various retailers who stock that model. These will provide information on both hardware and software supplied with that model. In addition, you will find links to other sites which provide drivers and user forums where you can see the problems and fixes that other users have encountered.

There's lots of help online

Whatever problem you are experiencing, somebody, somewhere has probably been through it and posted the results on the Web. You can't always trust everything you see on the Web, of course, but you can often find some useful pointers.

The same logic applies to individual components. For instance, if you need new drivers for (say) your graphics card, an Internet search on the manufacturer's name and any serial number that you find on the card will produce several pages of information. The problem, generally, is the sheer volume of information that you have to work through to find what you want. For example a search on the term GeForce 8400 GS produced over a million results. However, the first page of results produces the information that this is an nVidia card (the manufacturer's site came top of the search results list), gives details of suppliers if you want to buy one and included product reviews from other users.

YOUR PC HARDWARE

You can, of course, remove the cover and look for yourself in order to see what components are in the box and how they are laid out. What type of hard disk do you have; a parallel connector or serial ATA? Do you have any spare RAM slots for a memory upgrade? (You may find it useful to look at Chapter 7 before trying this.)

WINDOWS

From the **Start** button, navigate to Control Panel > System and Security > System. Alternatively use the Search facility in the **Start** menu to search on System. Whichever route you choose you will see something like this:

This provides basic information about your PC. Note the version of Windows that you are using (in this case Home Premium) and the link 'Get more features....'. Clicking on this link will open 'Windows Anytime Upgrade', from here you may upgrade to a more powerful version of Windows by purchasing an upgrade licence or by entering an upgrade key that you have already bought.

Other items of note are information about the processor type, the amount of installed RAM and the operating system type (32-bit or 64-bit). Clicking on the Change Settings link will open the System Properties; from here you can view/change many aspects of your PC – its name, the Workgroup of which it is a member, visual effects and so on. We'll return to this set of tools later in the book, but for now treat it as a source of useful information.

> You can run a 32-bit version of Windows on a 64-bit machine with very little loss of performance. You cannot run a 64-bit version of Windows on 32-bit hardware.

You can also obtain more detailed information by launching a CMD prompt and typing 'systeminfo' + [Enter]. If you do this, you will see something like:

Even if it is not much direct use to you at this stage, it is useful to know how to use a command prompt to produce information that can be placed in a text file and sent, if necessary, to a third party.

It probably took you more than ten minutes to do all that but if you have completed the tasks outlined you now have a sound background knowledge of your system and will be able to get a lot more out of the rest of the book.

```
C:\Windows\system32\cmd.exe                                    [_] [□] [X]

Microsoft Windows [Version 6.1.7600]
Copyright (c) 2009 Microsoft Corporation.  All rights reserved.

C:\Users\Anthony>systeminfo

Host Name:                 BURGESS-7
OS Name:                   Microsoft Windows 7 Home Premium
OS Version:                6.1.7600 N/A Build 7600
OS Manufacturer:           Microsoft Corporation
OS Configuration:          Standalone Workstation
OS Build Type:             Multiprocessor Free
Registered Owner:          Anthony
Registered Organization:
Product ID:                00359-OEM-8992607-00010
Original Install Date:     19/02/2010, 12:38:36
System Boot Time:          23/02/2010, 08:15:45
System Manufacturer:       System Manufacturer
System Model:              System Name
System Type:               X86-based PC
Processor(s):              1 Processor(s) Installed.
                           [01]: x86 Family 6 Model 6 Stepping 2 AuthenticAMD ^
666 Mhz
BIOS Version:              Award Software, Inc. ASUS A7V8X-X ACPI BIOS Revision
1012, 22/07/2004
Windows Directory:         C:\Windows
System Directory:          C:\Windows\system32
Boot Device:               \Device\HarddiskVolume1
System Locale:             en-gb;English (United Kingdom)
Input Locale:              en-gb;English (United Kingdom)
Time Zone:                 (UTC) Dublin, Edinburgh, Lisbon, London
Total Physical Memory:     2,048 MB
Available Physical Memory: 1,425 MB
Virtual Memory: Max Size:  4,095 MB
Virtual Memory: Available: 3,350 MB
Virtual Memory: In Use:    745 MB
Page File Location(s):     C:\pagefile.sys
Domain:                    WORKGROUP
Logon Server:              \\BURGESS-7
Hotfix(s):                 14 Hotfix(s) Installed.
                           [01]: KB971468
                           [02]: KB972270
                           [03]: KB974332
                           [04]: KB974431
                           [05]: KB974571
                           [06]: KB975467
                           [07]: KB975560
                           [08]: KB976898
                           [09]: KB977074
                           [10]: KB978207
                           [11]: KB978251
                           [12]: KB978262
                           [13]: KB978506
                           [14]: KB979099
Network Card(s):           3 NIC(s) Installed.
                           [01]: Broadcom 802.11g Network Adapter
                                 Connection Name: Wireless Network Connection
                                 Status:          Media disconnected
                           [02]: VIA Rhine II Compatible Fast Ethernet Adapter
                                 Connection Name: Local Area Connection
                                 Status:          Media disconnected
                           [03]: Realtek RTL8139/810x Family Fast Ethernet NIC
                                 Connection Name: Local Area Connection 2
                                 DHCP Enabled:    Yes
                                 DHCP Server:     192.168.2.1
                                 IP address(es)
                                 [01]: 192.168.2.101
                                 [02]: fe80::b90a:8559:bae8:bfff
```

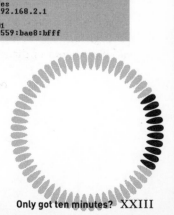

1

Maintaining Windows

In this chapter you will learn:
- *about Windows versions*
- *four maintenance things you can do now*
- *about Safe Mode*
- *how to use the Repair your Computer option*

Windows versions

This book is written in terms of Windows 7 Home Premium Edition; this is the most frequently used version of Windows for home users. The book assumes that you are familiar with the basics of using Windows. If you are not, or you need a primer on Windows 7 – try *Teach Yourself Get Started in Windows 7*.

WINDOWS 7

Windows 7 comes in several different versions, some of which are only available in certain territories, for licensing and legal reasons. For most of us the choices are between:

- *Windows 7 Home Premium*
- *Windows 7 Professional*
- *Windows 7 Ultimate*

These are available in both 32-bit and 64-bit versions. A 32-bit version will run on a 64-bit processor, but a 64-bit version will not run on a 32-bit processor.

System requirements for running Windows 7 are:

- ▶ *1 gigahertz (GHz) or faster 32-bit (×86) or 64-bit (×64) processor*
- ▶ *1 gigabyte (GB) RAM (32-bit) or 2 GB RAM (64-bit)*
- ▶ *16 GB available hard disk space (32-bit) or 20 GB (64-bit)*
- ▶ *Direct × 9 graphics device with WDDM 1.0 or higher driver.*

WINDOWS VISTA

Windows Vista is the immediate forerunner of Windows 7. The hardware requirements to run it are only slightly less than Windows 7 so an upgrade is probably feasible. If you are considering an upgrade there is an upgrade advisor tool that can be downloaded from:

http://www.microsoft.com/windows/windows-7/get/upgrade-advisor.aspx

If you don't want to upgrade to Windows 7 you will find that most of the features in this book will work if you are using Vista.

WINDOWS XP

XP is now a 'mature' system. Consequently it lacks many of the advanced features of the later versions. However, if you are still using XP, many of the features in this book will work, though you may have to do a bit of head scratching and puzzling before you get a result.

Four things you can do now

PC systems tend to slow down through time for various reasons. Moreover, they are often set up to give the most attractive appearance at the expense of performance, and this can be significant if you have an older or relatively low-powered PC.

Before you start, consider the safety and integrity of your data. The tools you are about to use are safe and reliable and have been in use by millions of users for many years. However, things do go wrong very occasionally. For example, a mains power failure part way through a disk defragmentation could cause data loss or corruption.

As a rule, it is wise to back up data and make a note of settings before doing any maintenance work. See Chapter 6 for more information on this. Having backed up your data (or decided to accept the small risk of not doing so) we can get down to business with the operating system tools.

Note: some of the utilities on some systems may require you to have Administrator rights to use them. If, when you try to access a utility, you receive an error message along the lines of 'You do not have sufficient rights to …' Right-click on the program icon and select 'Run as Administrator' from the context menu.

CHECK DISK

Like many Windows utilities, Check Disk can be accessed through several routes. Space limitations mean that it is not possible to describe them all here. Perhaps the easiest way is to select the disk you wish to check, then select from the Tools menu. To run Check Disk:

1 *Click (or double-click) on* **Computer** *(right-hand side of the Start menu).*
2 *Right-click on the C: drive and select* **Properties.**
3 *Select the* **Tools** *tab.*
4 *Click* **Check Now.**

The figure shows the Check Disk utility. Click **Start** to begin. If you leave the two option boxes unchecked, Check Disk will simply check the file system for errors. More thorough testing can be done by selecting either or both of the checkboxes. Depending on the choice you make, you may have to restart the machine. If you do this, the disk will be checked as the PC starts up and you will see a (probably unfamiliar) text-based screen – white characters on a blue screen – which will report progress and, when complete, continue the boot process to the usual Desktop.

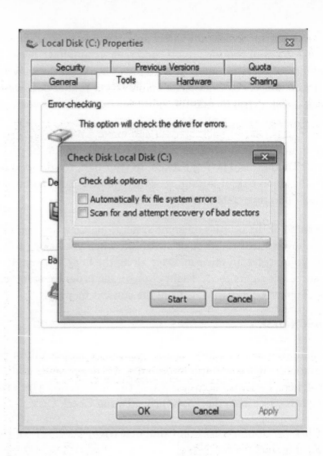

The Disk Cleanup Wizard

Hard disks accumulate rubbish files through time – temporary files from application installers and the Internet are probably the worst culprits. These files take up disk space and, especially if the disk is fairly full, can slow the system down substantially. The Disk Cleanup Wizard is the Windows utility to deal with these unwanted files and it is available in all Windows versions.

1 *Click on* **My Computer.**
2 *Right-click on the C: drive and select* **Properties.**

3 *Select the* **General** *tab.*
4 *Click* **Disk** *Cleanup.*

The system will spend a few seconds gathering information and will then present you with some options.

(Note the button for Clean up system files.)

5 *Accept the default values, or change them by checking or unchecking boxes.*
6 *When you have made your choices click* **OK**. *You will be asked 'Are you sure you want to permanently delete these files?' – Click the* **Delete Files** *button if you do.*

The system will then display its progress and offer the option to cancel until it is finished.

The Disk Defragmenter

Imagine a library where returned books are placed on the first available shelf space and the catalogue is updated to record their new position. After a while, books would be shelved all over the place, and something like a multi-volume encyclopaedia would take a long time to find because the individual volumes would be on different shelves or even different floors of the building.

Windows stores files rather like the books in the library example. When a file is written to the hard disk it is written to the first available storage unit (cluster). A large file may be written across several clusters and these may be widely separated. When files are deleted it makes more clusters available, possibly in the middle of other files. This is known as fragmentation and the answer to the problem is defragmentation: that is, rearranging the storage clusters so that all parts of the same file are on the same part of the hard disk, making them easier to find and quicker to load.

Finding programs

As with many utilities and programs in Windows 7 you can use the 'traditional' route through the menu system or you can use the Search facility.

For example, navigate to the disk defragmenter by the traditional route:

1 Right-click on **Computer**.
2 Right-click on **C: Drive**.
3 Select **Properties > Tools**.
4 Click the **Defragment now** button.

Alternatively, type 'defragment' in to the Search box on the **Start** menu and select the Defragmentation utility from the list.

Whichever route you choose you will see a panel which looks like this:

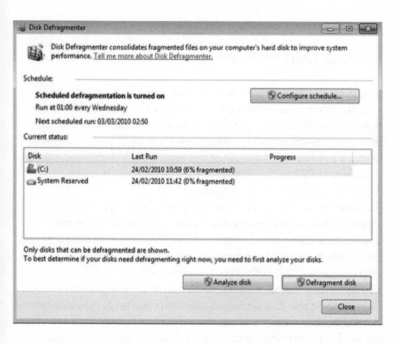

As you can see from the figure, there are three buttons: **Configure schedule**, **Analyze disk** and **Defragment disk**.

▶ **Configure schedule.** *If you click on the* **Configure schedule** *button you will be presented with a dialog box that gives you the tools to schedule a regular defragmentation session.*
▶ **Analyze disk.** *This option calculates the level of fragmentation of the disk and recommends that you carry out a defrag if the level of defragmentation warrants it.*
▶ **Defragment disk.** *This carries out a defragmentation irrespective of the level of fragmentation on the disk.*

Defragmentation of a large disk can be a time-consuming business. You can continue working as the defrag utility works in the background but this will slow things down even further so there is case to be made for setting up a regular schedule – to run at a time when the machine is on but not in use – and forget about it.

Visual Effects

Windows is designed to be visually attractive, with 3-D buttons, sliding or fading menus and other visual effects. If you like these features and you have a reasonably powerful machine to support them, fine. However, if you want to release some processing power you can modify these special effects through the Windows interface.

To change the visual effects settings:

1 *Right-click on* **Computer** *and select* **Properties** *from the context menu.*
2 *Click on the* **Change Settings** *link near the bottom right of the page.*
3 *Select the* **Advanced** *tab.*
4 *Click on the first* **Settings** *button (the one under the heading of Performance).*

The figure shows the Visual Effects settings in Windows 7. They are set to the default value of **Let Windows Choose** and in this instance it has chosen settings which are the same as the **Best Appearance** settings. Selecting **Best Performance** will disable all of the visual effects. **Custom settings** allows you to choose the combination of visual effects that you want by checking or unchecking the appropriate boxes. The best way to decide what you want is simply to experiment. If you don't like the results, you can always change them back!

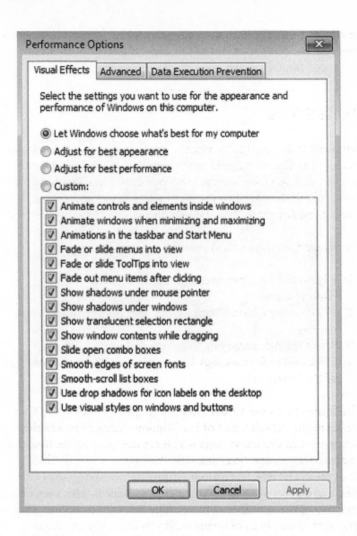

Using Safe Mode

Safe Mode is a special diagnostic mode of Windows which loads
and runs the operating system with the minimum of drivers. It
is sometimes possible to boot to Safe Mode when a machine won't

otherwise start. The easiest way to start Safe Mode is to hold down [F8] as the system boots up. This takes you to Windows' Advanced Boot Options:

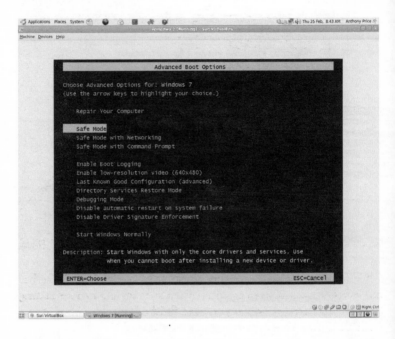

At this screen, select **Safe Mode** and press [Enter]. The system will continue to run in white on black text mode and you can watch the drivers being loaded. This may take a while.

When all drivers are loaded you will be presented with a graphical desktop.

Note that Windows displays the Help file for Safe Mode on the right of the Desktop and that the corners of the display show the words 'Safe Mode' to remind you that this is not a normal working mode.

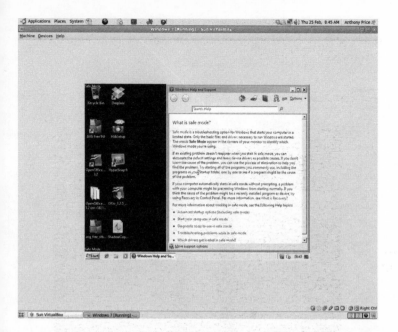

Once you are in Safe Mode you can fix any problems that may be hindering the normal boot process such as incorrect display settings or corrupted drivers. When you have finished simply reboot as normal.

Using the Repair your Computer option

If you cannot fix your problems by using Safe Mode there is a Repair option in the Advanced Boot menu which requires you to select a language-specific keyboard and to log in using your password. If you do this you will be presented with the **System Recovery** options.

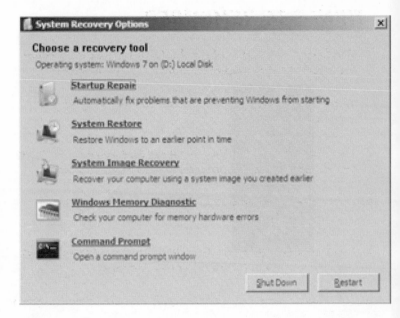

- ► **Startup Repair** *is an automated repair option. Clicking on this will cause Windows to attempt to repair itself without any further input from you.*
- ► *The* **System Restore** *and* **System Image Recovery** *options are described in Chapter 2.*
- ► *The* **Windows Memory Diagnostic** *utility checks for hardware faults in system RAM and the Command Prompt opens a command-prompt Window.*

With luck you may never need to use any of these tools.

THINGS TO REMEMBER

1 *Windows 7 needs 1 Gb of RAM (2Gb for the 64-bit version) but where RAM is concerned: more is better – always!*

2 *32-bit versions of Windows will run on a 64-bit system but not vice versa.*

3 *The Search box on the Start menu can save you a lot of typing and clicking to find the program or utility that you want.*

4 *Defragmentation can be a long job. It's best to automate it with the Scheduler.*

5 *Fancy graphics and effect use a lot of processing power. They can be tamed if not turned off in their entirety.*

6 *Safe Mode makes it possible to repair a misconfigured graphics display.*

7 *The Repair your Computer option provides tools to attempt an automated repair of a broken Windows installation.*

2

....

Backups and system images

In this chapter you will learn:
- *how to make a repair disk*
- *about backups*
- *how to use System Restore*
- *about shadow copies of files*

Windows 7 provides a number of backup tools which means that you can back up your data, your settings, or even your entire installed system. Obviously, there is no point in having a backup unless you have the means to restore it and one of the tools for restoring a system is a repair disk. This is a bootable CD which provides much the same facilities as Safe Mode/Repair option (see Chapter 1) on a system that is otherwise unbootable. The utility to make a repair disk is part of the backup system. As with many features in Windows there is more than one way of starting it:

Either: Click on Control Panel in the **Start** menu and navigate to System and **Security > Backup your computer > Create a system repair disk**

Or: type 'backup' in the Search box on the **Start** menu and select from the results

Or: type 'repair' in the Search box on the **Start** menu and select from the results.

MAKING A REPAIR DISK

For this, you will need a blank, writeable CD and a working CD drive.

1 *Start the Create Repair Disk utility. You will see a dialog box that looks like this:*

2 *Put a blank writeable CD in the drive and click on the* **Create disc** *button. The system will take a couple of minutes to prepare the necessary files and burn them to the CD that you have provided. When it has finished you will see something like:*

3 *Label the disk and store it somewhere safe. With luck you may never need it but it is as well to be prepared.*

> Repair disks are not specific to the systems on which they are made but if you have both 32-bit and 64-bit systems you should make a separate version for each type.

Backups

A backup is simply a copy of some files that exists independently of the system on which they were made and which can be restored if the originals are lost or corrupted. Whether you back up user files or the entire system; whether the medium is CD/DVD or a hard disk, the backup should be stored securely as far away as possible from the system itself, ideally in a different room or even a different building. We will consider only 'local' media but the techniques outlined in this chapter can also be used over a network.

SETTING UP THE BACKUP UTILITY

This only needs to be done once though you can, of course, change the settings later if you wish. To set up the backup system, open the Backup utility. You will see something like this:

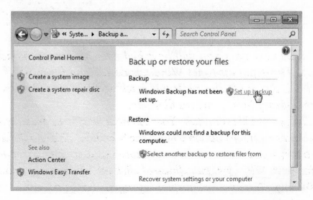

1 *Click on the* **Set up backup** *link. Windows will search for suitable media and list them. This will include removable media such as writeable CDs/DVDs or hard disks which may be removable or fixed inside the PC. Obviously for a backup, a removable hard disk is better than built-in, but built-in is better than nothing.*
2 *Choose your backup destination from the list.*

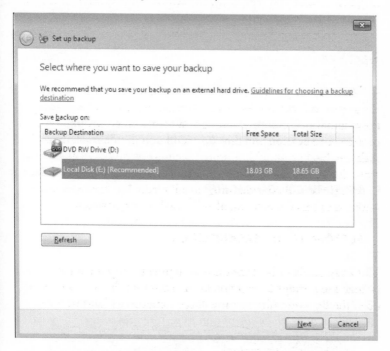

3 *At the next stage you will be asked what you want to back up. The default is to let Windows decide and for most of us this is a sensible choice. It will back up your user files ignoring temporary files, program files, etc.*
4 *Click on the* **Next** *button. You will now be able to review your choices. Note the option to* **Edit the Schedule**. *This should be set to perform a backup (say) once a week so that you can set and forget it. When you have finished click on* **Save Settings and Run Backup**. *Windows will display a progress bar as it works and confirm its completion.*

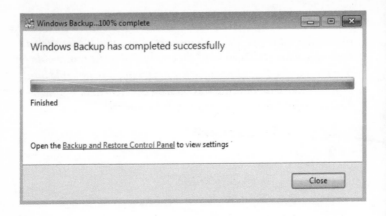

From now on Windows will perform a backup according to your specification and schedule until you decide to change things.

RESTORING FROM BACKUP

This is essentially the reverse of the backup process.

1 *Start the Backup utility.*
2 *Select the files and folders that you want to restore – all users, all your own files or selected files and folders.*
3 *Having made your choices click on the **Next** button. You will now be given the option to restore files to their original location (the default) or to choose a new location.*
4 *Having made your choice, click on the **Restore** button. If there are any conflicts between files the system will inform you and you can choose what to do about them.*

Note the checkbox – bottom left – which enables you to automate your responses.

5 *Once you have told the system how to resolve any conflicts it will run to completion without further user intervention.*

System images

A system image is a byte-by-byte copy of your system. It includes the operating system itself (Windows 7) and installed applications such as Office, Acrobat Reader, etc. A system image can be created on a hard disk (preferably a removable disk) or on one or more writeable DVDs. Note that this is an all-or-nothing proposition; you can't select individual files or folders; all you can do is create or restore a whole image.

CREATING A SYSTEM IMAGE

1 *Navigate to the Backup utility and click on the link* **Create a System Image.** *Windows will scan for suitable media. In this instance we have a choice of creating our image on either a local hard disk (E:) or writing to one or more DVDs.*

2 *Whichever option you choose you will need to boot to a repair disk in order to restore a broken system.*

3 *Having selected your destination drive click on* **Next.** *The next screen indicates the drives to be included (by default C: and a small reserved system partition). Accept – or make changes as you wish – then click on* **Next,** *then* **Start backup.** *Windows will begin to create the system backup. After a while, it will prompt for a writeable DVD:*

4 Label a suitable DVD and put it in the drive, then click on **OK**.

5 You will now be prompted to format the disk. Click on **Format**. Windows will format the disk and start the backup process. This a longish job – an ideal time for coffee break or a sandwich.

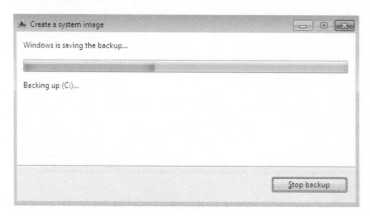

6 When the imaging process is complete, Windows will indicate this and prompt you to create a repair disk if you need one. Close the backup system and remove the disk from the drive.

RESTORING A SYSTEM IMAGE

Unfortunately, the image disk that you created is not bootable so in order to restore the image you need to boot to a repair disk before putting the image disk in the drive.

To restore from a saved image:

1 Boot the target system to a repair disk. This can take a couple minutes.

2 Set the language for the keyboard to suit your region (the default is US) then click on **Next**. Windows will detect the installed system.

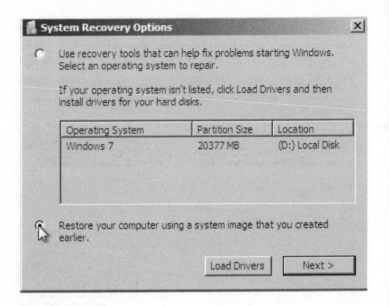

3 *Click the radio button to* **Restore From an Image** *(bottom left of the box) and click on* **Next.** *You will now receive a warning that Windows cannot find an image file.*

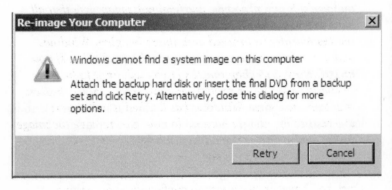

4 *Remove the Repair Disk from the drive and replace it with the image disk. Click on* **Retry.** *If you can't see the image disk immediately give it a few seconds then click on* **Refresh.** *You will see something like:*

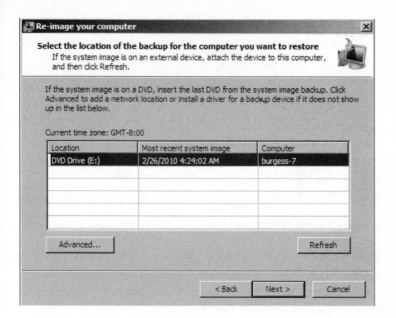

5 *Select the image that you want to restore and click on* **Next**.
Continue clicking on the **Next** *button at each screen then click
on* **Finish**. *You will receive one final notice warning that all
data will be replaced and asking if you want to continue. Click
on* **Yes** *in order to proceed with the re-imaging. Windows
will now restore your saved image to the hard drive. If you
image spans more than one DVD you will need to be there
to change disks when prompted; apart from that the process
is automatic. When Windows has finished it will restart
automatically. All you have to do now is to remove the image
disk from the drive, store it somewhere safe and test drive
your newly restored system.*

Once you have a newish system configured and working
how you want it, make an image. Then, when Windows
begins to slow down with use, and all else fails to speed it up
again, you can return to a 'clean build'. Some performance-
minded people do this two or three times a year as a matter
of routine.

System Restore

System Restore is concerned only with system files. Its operation is the same in all Windows versions. Word processing files, pictures, e-mails and other data files are not affected by this utility. This means that you need to back these items up for yourself using the Backup utility that comes with Windows or by one of the alternatives outlined in Chapter 6. The good side of this is that if you do need to 'roll back' your system to an earlier date, you won't lose your data.

RESTORING YOUR SYSTEM

There are several routes to the System Restore utility. You can navigate to the Control Panel (see Chapter 3 for a more detailed examination of the Control Panel), by searching on 'restore' through the Start menu or like this:

1   *Right-click on the* **Computer** *entry in the* **Start** *menu and select* **Properties** *from the context menu. This will take you to part of the Control Panel:*

2   *Click on the link to* **System Protection,** *then click on the* **System Restore** *button. This displays a panel:*

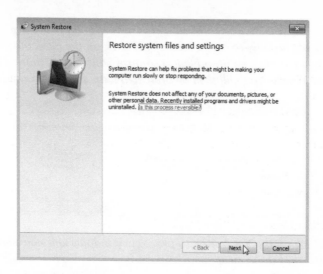

3 Click on **Next**. *Windows will now list the available restore points.*

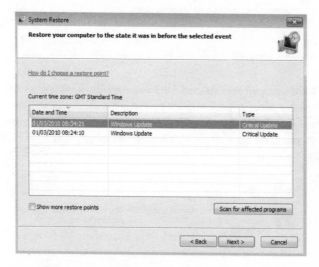

Note that there are options to show other restore points and to check the impact of using a particular restore point on your installed programs.

4 *When you have established which restore point is best for your needs (usually the most recent one) click on the* **Next** *button. You will then be prompted to confirm your restore point. Click on* **Finish.** *You will then be presented with a final warning:*

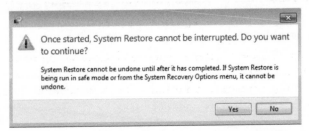

5 *Click on the* **Yes** *button to proceed. Windows will now start the shut-down process.*

6 *Windows will reboot and output progress messages as the Restore process proceeds. When it is finished you will be presented with the usual login procedures (or none if your system is set up that way). Finally, Windows will confirm the Restoration.*

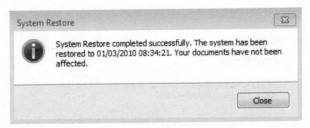

7 *Click on* **Close** *and continue using your restored system.*

SETTING YOUR OWN RESTORE POINTS

Although Windows makes a pretty good job of saving your settings, it may be prudent to set a restore point of your own before doing a job such as a major software installation. To set a restore point:

1 *Navigate to* **System Properties** > **System Restore** *and click on the* **Create** *button. You will be prompted for a name for your restore point.*

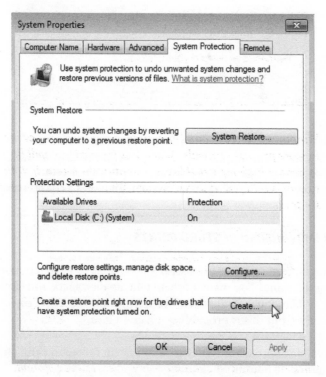

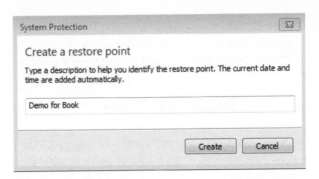

2 *Enter a name and click on the* **Create** *button. Windows will create a new restore point (this can take several minutes) and will confirm completion when it has finished.*

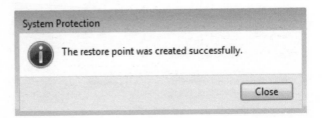

3 *Click on* **Close** *and continue using your system.*

You can step through the first few steps of the Restore process – see Restoring Your System, above – to confirm that your restore point is there.

REMOVING OLD RESTORE POINTS

Although restore points are useful it is possible to have too much of a good thing. Too many of them take up disk space and slow your system down. You can, off course, turn off System Protection altogether, but this is probably not a good idea.

A possible approach is to navigate to System Protection and click on the **Delete** button.

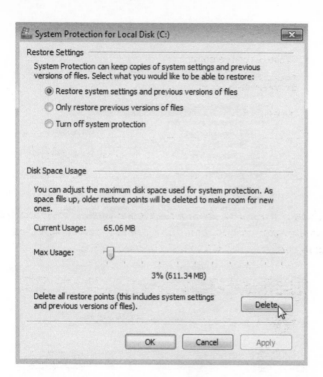

This will delete ALL restore points so if you choose this option be sure to create a new restore point of your own immediately afterwards.

Alternatively, you can use the Disk Cleanup utility to remove all restore points except the last one. As always there is more than one route to this utility, the easiest being to type 'cleanmgr' in the Search box on the **Start** menu then clicking on the Cleanmgr Program entry in the list.

Whichever way you start it, the Disk Cleanup Utility will do some calculations then present you with a panel like this:

1 *Click on the* **Clean up system files** *button. Windows will go through another calculation routine and then present you with the next screen. Choose the* **More Options** *tab.*

2 *Click on the* **Clean up** *button in the lower half of the panel. Windows will ask you to confirm.*

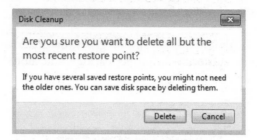

3 *Click on* **Delete** *to proceed. This will remove all previous restore points except the last one.*

Shadow copies

Every time that Windows makes a restore point it also makes shadow copies of your user files. This means that you can restore an individual user file from the Restore system.

1 *Right-click on the file icon and select* **Restore previous versions** *from the context menu.*

2 *This will list previous versions of the file that have been saved as part of the restore Points. Click on the old version that you require – there's only one in this example – and it will be restored.*

Useful though it may be in an emergency, the Shadow copy system is no substitute for proper backups and should not be relied upon.

THINGS TO REMEMBER

1 *A backup is simply a copy of some files which exists independently of the system where they were created. Useful though they may be, shadow copies on your system are not independent.*

2 *Techniques outlined in this chapter have been illustrated by reference to local disks and storage. They apply equally well to a network system.*

3 *A Repair Disk is bootable. A system image disk (or disk set) is not.*

4 *You can set your own restore points in addition to those created by Windows.*

5 *You can remove unwanted restore points to save space and improve performance.*

6 *You can locate a program – such as Backup – by typing its name in the Search box on the Start menu.*

7 *You an add a program to the Start menu or the Taskbar by right-clicking on its name and choosing the appropriate option from the context menu.*

8 *Because the entries in the Start menu and Taskbar are shortcuts you can remove them without affecting the installed programs.*

3

Control Panel

In this chapter you will learn:
- *how to access the Control Panel*
- *about the basic functions of the Control Panel tools*
- *how to personalize your system*

The Control Panel has been a feature of Windows systems over several editions. The version that is part of Windows 7 is the most comprehensive to date. If you click on the Control Panel entry in the Start menu you will see something like this:

This is the Windows default 'Category view'. At the top right corner there is a Search box which means that you can search for any item within the Control Panel. The search engine uses keywords rather than program names. For instance if you type 'backup' in the search box you will see:

Note that the search has identified not just the backup program, but associated topics such as Restore and System Restore. There is also a link to the wider Windows Help system. There are Back and Forward arrows (top left) and a drop-down list of previous locations:

Wherever you are in the Control Panel you never more than a click or two away from Home.

If you switch from the default Category View to one of the icon views you will see a full list of Control Panel items which you can click and use. Some people prefer this view; it is really just a matter of what suits your way of working.

This figure shows the Small Icon View of the Control Panel. Whichever view you prefer (and you can swap between them as you wish) the icon view gives a good indication of the range of utilities that Windows provides.

> You can see an interesting list view by searching Control Panel on a single letter such as 'a' or 's' – give it a try!

HOW THE CONTROL PANEL WORKS

Because the Control Panel is indexed on key words there are many cross-references within its structure. This supports a task-oriented approach to using it. For example, if you wish to change the time shown by the system clock you could search the Control Panel for the word 'time'.

> You can search for a term such as 'time' in the Start menu but this will show entries under the headings of Programs, Control Panel and Documents. For a common keyword this will generate a large list. A search on the term in the Control Panel will be restricted to the Control Panel and is therefore better focused.

THE CONTROL PANEL SEARCH UTILITY IN ACTION

Search term: 'time'. Results:

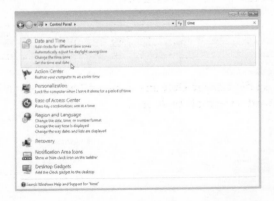

The obvious candidate here is the **Set the time and date** entry under the main **Date and Time** heading. Before clicking on this, note for future reference the variety of Time-related topics listed. We will return to some of these later in the chapter.

Clicking on the **Set the time and Date** entry opens the Date and Time panel which shows the current settings.

Clicking on the **Change Date and Time** button opens another panel which provides the tools to do this.

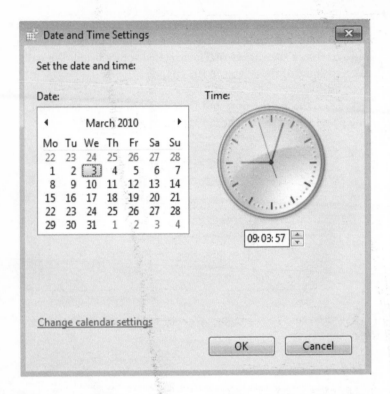

Make your changes – or click on **Cancel** if you are just exploring – and you will return to the main Date and Time panel. Note that there are also options to change the time zone and to enable (or disable) daylight saving. Note, too, that there are additional tabs for setting up additional clocks and synchronizing your system time with an Internet time server.

EXPLORING THE CONTROL PANEL

Now that you know how the Control Panel works and how to change between Category and Icon views of its contents you can explore the utilities that if offers. The system is too big to catalogue all of it here and some advanced features are mainly of interest to System Administrators. The remainder of the chapter concentrates the features of interest to the home user.

System and Security

This figure shows the Category View of the System and Security topic.

THE ACTION CENTER

This provides information on the system and the tools to change the settings that it reports. For example, clicking on the Review option will show something like this.

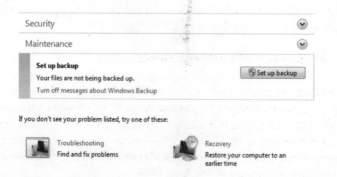

As you can see from the figure, there are two drop-down lists which enable you to examine – and if necessary change – **Security** and **Maintenance** settings. The only problem reported in this instance is that the Backup system has not been set up. Having provided the information about the problem, Windows also provides the tools to fix it, in this case a button, **Set up Backup**.

Before leaving the Action Center note and/or explore the other topics listed there:

▶ *Change User Account Control Settings – fine-tune your system to determine what warnings are issued in what circumstances (the defaults are okay for most users)*
▶ *Troubleshoot common problems*
▶ *Restore your computer to an earlier time – a link to the System Restore utility.*

WINDOWS FIREWALL

By default the firewall is ON and is configured to notify you when it blocks a program from accessing the Net. The default settings are best for most users though you can, of course, change them. Note that there is an option to restore defaults if you make a change and are not happy with it.

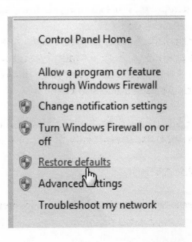

SYSTEM

The default view of the System shows details of the system:

- ▶ *Windows edition*
- ▶ *Processor type*
- ▶ *Amount of installed (RAM) memory*
- ▶ *Computer name*
- ▶ *Workgroup name*

Note that there is a link, **Change Settings**, which will open
the tools needed to change these settings. Note, too, that Windows
activation status is 'Activated' and that the Microsoft Genuine
badge confirms that this is a licensed copy.

The menu on the left of the default view includes links to other
features. The first of these is especially important as it leads to:

DEVICE MANAGER

This provides access to all attached hardware. If the list is closed up –
as in the figure – there are no problems with your hardware.

You can open up any list element and Windows will provide information about current device drivers for the device, a button to update drivers and a button to uninstall the device.

Where a device is causing problems uninstalling and reinstalling can often provide a quick fix.

WINDOWS UPDATE

Like all operating systems, Windows is under constant revision and improvement. Updates are available over the Internet and

the update service is turned on by default. You can also
check manually if new updates are available by clicking on
the **Check for updates** link and you can also list previously
downloaded and installed updates by clicking the **View Installed
Updates** link.

POWER OPTIONS

The power options are set up by default to strike a balance
between power saving and performance and are suitable for most
users. There is also provision to change the behaviour of the
physical buttons on your hardware – you can for example
disable the power button so that the PC can only be shut
down through the Windows operating system – or modify the
behaviour of the Sleep button if it is present. There is also an
option to require a password when the system resumes from a
Sleep state.

BACKUP AND RESTORE

These options have been examined at length in Chapter 2.

WINDOWS ANYTIME UPGRADE

This is an online service that enables you to buy an upgrade to a
more powerful version of Windows. An upgrade of this type does
not require you to reinstall Windows. All you do is buy a new
licence key, enter it and reboot. The enhanced features are now
enabled and you can use them just as if this were a new install
of the more powerful Windows version.

ADMINISTRATIVE TOOLS

These are mainly tools for the commercial Systems Administrator
such as the Event Viewer or provide links to disk tools such as
Defragmentation (considered in Chapter 1) and Create and format
partitions which is covered in Chapter 8.

User Accounts and Family Safety

USER ACCOUNTS

Every user on a Windows system needs a user account. At least one account – yours – was set up when Windows was installed. This account has full Administrator rights: that is, you can change system settings, create and delete files and folders, etc. without restriction. If this account is not password-protected, then anyone who starts up your PC or laptop – with or without your knowledge or permission – has these abilities. This is an obvious security risk. To fix it, navigate to **Control Panel > User Accounts and Family Safety > User Accounts** and click on the link to **Create a password for your account**.

As the System Administrator you can change any aspect of your account: change your account picture, change your Windows password and manage the accounts of other users. You can see the options available to you in the figure.

PARENTAL CONTROLS

If you want to set up Parental Controls to restrict Internet access these cannot be applied to your own – or any other – account that has administrative rights. You need to create a new restricted account for a new user. You can do this through the User Accounts section of Control Panel or through a link in the Parental Controls section.

To set up a new account from the Parental Controls section:

1 *Click on the link to* **Set up Parental Controls for Any User**
2 *Click on* **Create New User Account**

3 *Give the account a name, check the box to require a password to be set when the account is first used and click on the* **Create account** *button. Windows will confirm the creation of the new user account.*

To set up Parental Controls on the new account:

1 *Click on the account icon and turn on the radio button to enforce current settings.*

2 *As you can see from the figure there are entries for:*
  ▷ *Time limits*
  ▷ *Games*
  ▷ *Program limits*

These are all 'Off' by default.

3 *Choose the activity that you wish to restrict, click on the link and make your choices. For example, if you want to restrict times of access, click on the Time limits link. You will see a grid like this:*

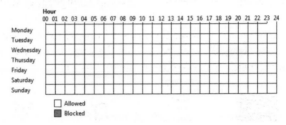

Control when Hilary will use the computer
Click and drag the hours you want to block or allow.

4 *Click on the squares that represent the times at which you want access to be denied. They will turn blue to represent being blocked. When you have made your choices, click on* **OK** *to confirm them.*
5 *Clicking on the* **Games** *link will give you choices to block all games or to selectively block games based on age ratings similar to film classifications or subject matter such as sex, drugs, violence, etc.*
6 *The* **Specific Programs** *option allows you to block access to particular applications on your PC.*

Network and Internet

The main headings in this section are:

▶ *Network and Sharing Center*
▶ *HomeGroup*
▶ *Internet Options*

The first two of these are covered in Chapters 17 and 18. Internet Options is covered in Chapter 15.

Appearance and Personalization

PERSONALIZATION

The Personalization option allows you to change the current
'theme' of your system, that is the desktop background, window
colour, sounds and screen saver that give your system its look and
feel. Clicking on the Change the Theme Link will show you the
available options and at the bottom of the screen you will see a
visual representation of the current theme, like this:

Desktop Background   Window Color   Sounds   Screen Saver
Solid Color   Windows 7 Basic   No Sounds   None

You can also change individual elements – such as desktop
background to create your own variation on any of the existing
themes.

DISPLAY

When Windows is installed, the display size is set to suit your
monitor and most people's preferences. This setting is a baseline
100%. The Display applet allows you to increase the size of your
screen elements to 125% or 150%. You will need to log off and
log on again for your changes to take effect.

DESKTOP GADGETS

These are marginally useful/decorative additions to your desktop
such as a clock, a currency converter, etc. To install a gadget,
double-click on it and it will install in the top right corner of your
display (or immediately under and gadget already displayed there).
Each gadget has a Close button so that you can remove it will a
single click.

TASKBAR AND START MENU

Clicking on this option opens a panel with three tabs.

▶ *From the* **Taskbar** *tab you can lock the Taskbar, autohide it, choose between standard and small icons or even change its position on screen.*

▶ *From the* **Start Menu** *tab you can customize the Start menu, with a button to restore default values if you don't like your changes.*

▶ *From the Toolbars tab you can choose which toolbars are displayed on the Taskbar.*

EASE OF ACCESS CENTER

This is a link to the Ease of Access Center that appears in the top level panel of the Control Panel. It provides tools to magnify screen images, to start a narrator which reads from the screen, start an on-screen keyboard and set up a high contrast display.

> If you turn on the on-screen keyboard and activate the narrator, the system will read out each letter as you press the key. Why not give it a try?

There are other options designed to increase the usability of the system for people with various disabilities but these are best approached in consultation with the intended end-user.

FOLDER OPTIONS

This applet has three tabs: General, View and Search.

▶ *The options available from the* **General** *tab are fairly self-explanatory. Try them and see what suits you and your way of working. There is a* **Restore Defaults** *button if you don't like the results of your changes.*
▶ *The* **View** *tab allows you to change such things as which files are visible in day-to-day use. By default, Windows doesn't display hidden or system files (not a bad idea for many users) and doesn't show file extensions. Thus the filename of the Word file* myfile.doc *is shown without its extension as* myfile. *If you wish to change these settings you can do so, safe in the knowledge that there is, once again, a* **Restore Defaults** *button.*
▶ *The* **Search** *tab allows you to modify the Windows search and indexing functions work. The default settings will suit most users but if you experiment and don't like the results there is a* **Restore Defaults** *button.*

FONTS

This enables you to display the installed fonts on your system. You can preview, delete, show or hide any of your fonts.

The screenshot shows a section of the preview of the Arial font. Note the Print button at the top which enables you to print hard copy of different sizes of the selected font.

Hardware and Sound

DEVICES AND PRINTERS

Adding a device 'by hand' is a rare occurrence in Windows 7. In the event of Windows not detecting a newly-attached device at boot time, clicking on the **Add a Device** link will start the hardware detection wizard. Once the hardware has been recognized, Windows will install appropriate drivers where possible including a search on the Internet for them if you are connected. If neither of these processes work, you may be prompted to provide drivers from a CD.

Sometimes it is necessary to override Windows automatic routines and force an install from the manufacturer's driver disk. We'll step through the process in the *Installing an ADSL (Broadband) Modem* topic in Chapter 15.

Adding a printer is accomplished by clicking on **Add Printer** to start the appropriate wizard. Again, in practice, you will seldom need to do this; Windows usually Plugs and Plays printers. Installing a printer is considered at more length in Chapter 11.

The **Mouse** link starts an applet that allows you to control all aspects of the mouse's behaviour.

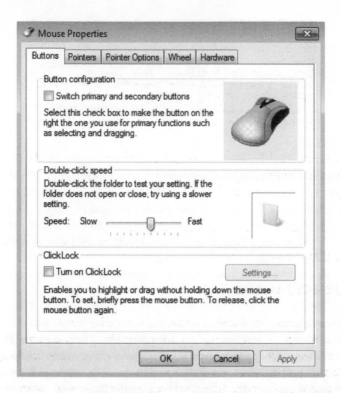

There are five tabs. The labels are pretty much self-explanatory. Try them and see.

There is also a link to Device Manager which we considered under the System heading earlier in the chapter.

AUTOPLAY

This feature allows you to control what Windows does when you insert removable media.

This feature is ON by default for all media and devices. For each device there is a drop-down list and you can select (for audio CD) 'Play', 'Open', 'Take no Action' or 'Ask every time'. Similar choices are offered for all other media and file types.

Choose what happens when you insert each type of media or device

☑ Use AutoPlay for all media and devices

Media

🔘 Audio CD

🔘 Enhanced audio CD

💿 DVD movie

Choose a default ▾
💿 Play audio CD using Windows Media Player
📁 Open folder to view files using Windows Explorer
🚫 Take no action
❓ Ask me every time

SOUND

The sound applet displays four tabs:

▶ **Playback** – *this controls the speaker system. If you click on the* **Configure** *button in this option you can test and adjust them. There is also a* **Properties** *button which enables you to control other settings including volume.*

▶ **Recording** – *this controls input sources such as microphone, line-in and phone line.*

▶ **Sounds** – *this gives you control over all system sounds. You can change entire sound schemes from a drop-down list or you can customize individual sound/event pairs. There is also a* **Test** *button so that you can check each sound effect before clicking on* **Apply** *to make the change permanent. You can even turn off system sounds altogether by choosing the* **No Sounds** *entry in the drop-down box. To disable Windows start-up sounds uncheck the* **Play Windows Startup Sound** *near the bottom of the page.*

▶ **Communications** – *enables you to set the behaviour of the system's volume when you receive (or make) an Internet phone call.*

POWER OPTIONS

These have already been examined under the *System* heading earlier in the chapter.

DISPLAY

Display options have been considered under the *Appearance and Personalization* heading earlier in the chapter.

Clock, language and region

DATE AND TIME

We have looked at the mechanics of setting date and time near the beginning of the chapter – see the material under the heading *The Control Panel search utility in action*.

REGION AND LANGUAGE

These settings are usually created when Windows is installed and seldom need to be changed. However, if you find that you have (for example) the wrong keyboard or currency settings for where you live you can adjust these and other settings using the Region and language applet.

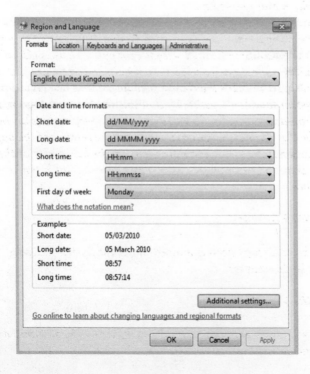

Programs

The most important headings here are:

Programs and features – install/uninstall applications and control Windows features

Default programs – enables you to set which programs open which types of file. For example, you may want to set Open Office to Open .doc files instead of opening them with Microsoft Word.

These are important utilities and are examined in detail in Chapter 12. The **Desktop Gadgets** heading has been examined as part of the *Appearance and Personalization* topic earlier in this chapter.

Ease of access

This topic has already been examined under that heading as part of the *Appearance and Personalization* section earlier in this chapter.

THINGS TO REMEMBER

1 *The Control Panel gives you access to all the major system utilities in one place.*

2 *The Control Panel has three views: Category, small icons and large icons. You can switch between views at any time.*

3 *Control Panel will remember the last view setting that you used next time you open it.*

4 *You can search the Control Panel in any view to find the utility that you need.*

5 *If you want to set up Parental Controls you need to create a non-privileged user account for this purpose.*

6 *Device Manager gives you a quick view of any hardware problems. If the list is closed all is well; if the list is opened up there is a problem.*

7 *Device Manager gives you a quick way to uninstall/reinstall drivers for problem hardware. This often provides a quick fix for hardware problems.*

8 *If your own privileged user account is not password-protected then any one with access to your PC or laptop can access all data and can change any system settings. If you don't have password protection in place you can fix this through the System and Security section of the Control Panel. (Hint: search on 'password' and Windows will show you the options.)*

4

Making a support call

In this chapter you will learn:
- **how to avoid making a support call (if you can)**
- **how to get the most for your money (if you can't)**
- **how to find a PC technician**

Before you call for Help

Sooner or later you will need to make a support call to a Help
Desk or look through the phone book or the small ads to find a PC
technician. Either of those options will cost you money, so before
you do anything, read this chapter.

Whether you are going to tackle the problem yourself or call
in an outsider – Help Desk or technician – the first thing to do
is to arm yourself with the facts after you have rebooted the
machine.

There are two reasons for this. First, simply closing the system
down and restarting it cures a lot of transient faults. The contents
of RAM (main system memory) are lost in the shutdown and
reloaded from scratch when you start up again. Second, if you
haven't rebooted, almost any Help Desk or technician will ask if
you have done this, so why pay an expert to tell you this when you
can simply do it yourself?

If the reboot doesn't work then you need to define the problem. The Help Desk operator or technician will ask you what the problem is and the clearer you are in your description the less time (and money) you will spend on a support call. Indeed, preparing to make a succinct fault report is often the first step to fixing the problem yourself. Describing – or preparing to describe – something to someone else can be a very effective way of organizing your own thinking.

Defining the problem

This need not be formal or complicated. What is necessary is to describe what happens or fails to happen. For example, 'I can't connect to the Internet' needs to be fleshed out a bit in order to be useful. Are you using a dialup modem connection or broadband? What, exactly do you do which causes the problem to manifest itself? A better description may be something like: 'When I click on the Internet Explorer icon on my Desktop, the modem begins to dial then, after half a minute I get an error message "remote host not responding"'.

A description along those lines makes it clear that the problem is with a dialup connection and suggests that the problem is probably with your Internet Service Provider – possibly their server is down for some reason.

Your best bet, in that scenario, would be simply to wait for an hour or two and try again later. Or, if you are in a hurry for a result, phone the ISP or use someone else's system to check the ISP's status page on the Web to see if there is a known problem. The following figure shows part of a status page from a UK-based ISP.

The support page gives details of known problems and provides a link to further Help. The same information could probably have been obtained through a single brief phone call to the ISP.

Service	Status		Next Update
Hosted Exchange:		Monitoring	05/03/10 15:00
Broadband:		Planned Maintenance	
Business Mobile:		Working	
Data/PC Backup:		Working	
Dial Up:		Working	
E-Store:		Working	
Email:		Working	

Gathering the information

Whoever you call for help, they will want to know the key facts about your system. It will save you time (and money) to have these facts to hand, so document them before you need them. Write them down and keep a print of the information somewhere safe. There's not much point in having your system details stored on a system that has stopped working! The information that you need might look something like that in Table 4.1.

You could extend this list almost indefinitely or gather more detail if you need or want it. A look at System Information, for example, would give a lot more detail, as shown in the figure on page 41.

Table 4.1

Item	Details	Source
PC manufacturer	DNUK	Documentation that came with the system Manufacturer's badge on case
CPU	AMD Athlon XP 2000 running at 1.67 GHz	Control Panel: System
Installed RAM	4 Gb	Control Panel: System

Item	Details	Source
Operating System	Windows 7 Home Premium	Control Panel: System
Disk Storage		
Hard Disk 1 Drive C:	20 Gb capacity with 10.6 Gb of free space NTFS File System	Properties of Computer – right-click on drive icon
Hard Disk 2 Drive F:	9.99 Gb capacity with 9.90 Gb free space NTFS File System	Properties of Computer – right-click on drive icon
Drives with removable storage	3.5" floppy drive 1 CD writer 1 DVD writer	Properties of Computer – right-click on drive icon or look at the front of the case!

Other useful information are e-mail and ISP login details. You will need to know/find out:

Table 4.2

Item	Details
ISP	UKLINUX
Dialup Number	08459042086
User Name	elenmar
Password	********
Incoming Mail Server	pop3.elenmar.com
Outgoing Mail Server	smtp.elenmar.com
Password	********

PASSWORDS

Write them down if you must, but NEVER tell anyone your password over the phone or by e-mail. If absolutely necessary, a password can be reset at your supplier's end. If this is necessary, log in as soon as possible afterwards and change it to something that is easy for you to remember but is hard for someone else to guess. It is good practice to use a mixture of upper and lower-case letters and numbers for a password, e.g. 'Frıday' is an easy to remember variant on 'friday' – easy to remember but hard to guess (at least, it was until somebody put it in a book!)

To find your user name for your Internet connection, just click on the icon that you generally use to connect to the Internet. The following figure shows details of an ADSL modem connection.

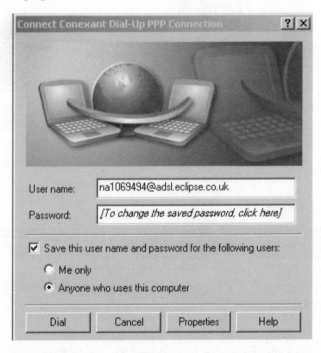

Your mail server settings can be obtained from your mail program. The standard mail client for Windows 7 is Windows Live Mail. To find the settings for that program:

1 *Click on the* **Windows Live Mail** *entry in the* **Start** *menu.*
2 *Right-click on the name of your mail account in the* **Live Mail** *menu, then select Properties from the context menu.*
3 *Select the* **Servers** *tab.*

4 *If – and only if – the box labelled* **My Server Requires**
Authentication *is ticked (as in the figure), you need to click*
Settings *which will take you to a further screen where you can*
enter separate account details and password for your outgoing
mail server. Most home users will not need to do this.

If you are not using Windows Live Mail, the procedure for
finding the information you require is much the same in other
mail clients such as Eudora or Thunderbird.

Calling the Help Desk

Many of the large High Street retailers offer some sort of warranty or support deal as part of the package. Typically, this requires you to call a Help Desk who will talk you through your problems. These calls are often expensive premium numbers so the more organized you are before you make the call the less it will cost.

Perhaps the most important thing is to have details of the system – make, model number, etc. – to hand along with details of any support contract or warranty you may have. With this in place, dial the number for the Help Desk, describe the problem to the operator and attempt to find a solution together.

Most Help Desk operators are helpful and knowledgeable about their own company's products and will talk you through the process of fixing things. However, they are usually working from a script and can only address a fairly limited range of problems. If, between you, you can't fix a problem fairly quickly, they may suggest running a Restore Disk – usually on one or two bootable CDs – which will restore the system to its original factory settings. Such a restore will destroy all of your data, and installed programs and settings. It may well fix your problem or, if it doesn't, it will have restored the factory defaults so that the Help Desk are now dealing with a machine whose configuration is known to them in detail.

Sometimes, a reinstall – known as 're-imaging' – is the best or even the only way of dealing with a problem. It is, however, a fairly drastic solution, so before doing it have a look at Chapter 13.

Finding a PC technician

Not everyone has a system which is covered by a warranty or a support contract so, if you can't fix the problem yourself, you will need to find a PC technician to do the job for you. There are three main sources of help for PC problems:

- ▶ *High Street names*
- ▶ *Local computer companies*
- ▶ *Sole traders – freelance technicians.*

THE HIGH STREET NAMES

These are the sort of household names that advertise on television and in national newspapers. Most of them offer support and extended warranty services for equipment bought from them. They also accept work from non-customers, but generally require you to take your PC to their premises or charge a hefty premium for a call out to your home. Their hourly rates are generally something like double those of the small local operator. The advantage of dealing with these companies is that they will (probably) still be there next year and that they have a reputation which they care about. They tend to do a good, if somewhat expensive, job. However, they are usually keen to try to sell you upgrades and extras that you may not really need.

A typical offer from one of these chains consists of doing the work – even if it's only a 'PC Health Check' for the quoted price – then advising that the machine 'could benefit from more RAM' and offer to fit it free if you pay for it while they still have the PC in their workshop. It's a fact of course, that just about any PC could benefit from more RAM – it's one of the most cost-effective upgrades that you can do yourself. A stick or two can be fitted in minutes and you can buy them online. The price from one of the High Street retailers is generally something like 30% more than you would pay for it online from the manufacturer: no wonder they can afford to spend two minutes fitting it 'free'.

LOCAL COMPUTER COMPANIES

A look through Yellow Pages or a local directory such as Thomson will generally list several local computer companies. These vary in size and the services they can offer. Like the High Street names they will probably advertise that their staff have various qualifications (more on qualifications later). The fact that they are in a directory indicates that they are established. They can offer the same advantages as their larger counterparts along with the same shortcomings – higher prices and trying to sell you upgrades you don't really need.

SOLE TRADERS

These independent operators will probably give you a better price than the larger companies, mainly because they have lower overheads. Most of them work from home or from small rented premises. When you buy from the High Street or the commercial/business park you are paying your share of the costs of the business rates, not to mention the costs of the glitzy premises.

The independent operators, at their best, can offer you a personal service in your own home for about half the price of the bigger companies. Many of them are skilled and experienced PC technicians; often they are employed in a school or a local authority and do a certain amount of freelance work as a sideline. A handful, though, are cyber cowboys, rip-off artists and clowns. So how do you know which is which?

Word-of-mouth recommendation from satisfied local customers is the best possible indication that someone is competent. If someone known to you can say 'Fred Bloggs did a good job for me' then there's a strong case for hiring Fred to do a job for you.

If no one you know can recommend a technician, then look in the small ads in the local paper or even the postcards in the newsagent's windows or notice boards in a local college. Before making the initial approach, consider the advert. Does it give an address and a landline number, or just a name and a mobile number? Does it say anything about qualifications, the services offered? Does the technician offer a 'no fix, no fee' service?

Having chosen perhaps two or three local techs, phone them and have a chat. Describe your problem in outline and ask if they can help. Ask what their hourly rate is, above all ask if they can give you names and contact details of (say) three local customers for whom they have worked in the past six months. And follow up on this. If you are dealing with a reputable, competent business there won't be a problem in obtaining and checking on customer references.

QUALIFICATIONS

Qualifications are no substitute for ability and experience, but they do matter. The basic qualification for a PC technician is the A+ Certificate from the Computing Technology Industry Association (CompTIA). CompTIA is a Chicago-based organization with members in 102 countries. Its corporate members include global household names like Intel and Microsoft. The A+ Certification is gained by taking two rigorous online examinations designed to test the knowledge of a PC technician with a minimum of six months' work experience. The examinations test the technician's knowledge of hardware, operating systems and the basics of networking. The content of the exams is updated every couple of years to reflect changes in the actual work carried out by CompTIA certified technicians who are working in the field. (Details of all CompTIA qualifications can be seen at their website www.comptia.org.)

There are other higher qualifications from companies such as Microsoft and Novell, but these are specific to those companies' own products. There are also, of course, various academic qualifications up to and including Master's degrees in information technology or computing. However, for a practical working tech, earning his or her living in the trade, CompTIA Certified PC Support Technician is about the best badge there is.

THINGS TO REMEMBER

1 *Always reboot your PC before trying to diagnose a fault.*

2 *Make (and keep up to date) a record of all your system settings. Keep copies away from your PC.*

3 *Define the problem. If you can describe it accurately you are halfway to solving it!*

4 *Have all your settings information available before you call the Help Desk. It will make your call shorter, more effective and cheaper.*

5 *When choosing a PC technician look for someone with CompTIA A+ Certification and (preferably) some satisfied local customers.*

5

The command line prompt

In this chapter you will learn:
- *how to access a command line*
- *the syntax of some common commands*
- *how to get help with commands*
- *how batch files and CMD scripts work*

Why use a command prompt?

All versions of Windows support the use of a command line prompt. This is often referred to as a 'DOS prompt' because of its similarity to the original, command-based, DOS operating system which powered the early PCs. Windows replaced DOS and its black and white command line some years ago, and these days we are all accustomed to the point-and-click simplicity of the Graphical User Interface (GUI). The command line, however, can still provide some useful tools for getting things done. A+ certified PC techs all have to be able to use a command line and, while it's not essential for the home user to be able to do so, it can be useful. If you want to, feel free to skip this chapter. If, on the other hand, you want to dig just a little deeper, read on.

Accessing a command line prompt

The command line prompt is one of the Accessories available from the Start menu on all Windows systems. To reach the prompt:

1 *In the* **Start** *menu, point to* **All Programs** *then* **Accessories**.
2 *Right-click on the* **Command Prompt** *entry in the menu. You will be given the option to* **Pin to Start Menu**. *You don't have to do this, to use the Command Prompt, but it can be handy to have that – or any other frequently-used item – pinned to the* **Start** *menu for quick access.*
3 *Click on the Command Prompt icon – whether you pinned it to the* **Start** *menu, made a shortcut to your Desktop, or navigated to it long hand – to launch the default Command Line Processor CMD.EXE.*

```
Command Prompt
Microsoft Windows [Version 6.1.7600]
Copyright (c) 2009 Microsoft Corporation.  All rights reserved.

C:\Users\Anthony>
```

The illustration shows a command line prompt in Windows 7. Note the version number 6.1.7600. The major version number – 6 – indicates that this is Windows version 6. The minor version number – 1 – tells us that this is the second release of Major Version 6 (the numbering starts from 0, which was Vista), and the third number – 7600 – indicates the 'build number' assigned to it by the system developers. All Windows releases use this numbering system to identify themselves.

DIRECTORIES AND FOLDERS

These are in fact the same thing. Where Windows refers to 'folders', which contain files (and other folders), the command prompt uses the term 'directory' which is a listing of the files (and subdirectories) which it contains.

By default, the command line prompt shows the current directory (or folder). Thus in the last figure we can see that the current directory is Anthony, a subdirectory of Users which is, in turn, a subdirectory of the root, indicated by the \ (backslash) character. The C: at the beginning tells us that this directory structure is on the first hard disk drive of the system.

Command syntax

Command syntax is simply the set of rules which govern the way in which a command is used. The general pattern is:

Command [options] [switches] Carriage Return

For example, if we want to see a list of all the files in the current directory, simply issue the command DIR at the prompt and follow it with a carriage return [CR] – (the [Enter] key).

The command DIR [CR] will produce output like this:

```
C:\Users\Anthony>DIR
 Volume in drive C has no label.
 Volume Serial Number is 54B7-1FBC

 Directory of C:\Users\Anthony

09/03/2010  08:19    <DIR>          .
09/03/2010  08:19    <DIR>          ..
20/02/2010  09:56    <DIR>          Contacts
08/03/2010  13:13    <DIR>          Desktop
08/03/2010  11:18    <DIR>          Documents
20/02/2010  09:56    <DIR>          Downloads
20/02/2010  09:57    <DIR>          Favorites
20/02/2010  10:14    <DIR>          Links
20/02/2010  09:56    <DIR>          Music
20/02/2010  09:56    <DIR>          Pictures
20/02/2010  09:56    <DIR>          Saved Games
20/02/2010  09:56    <DIR>          Searches
20/02/2010  09:56    <DIR>          Videos
               0 File(s)              0 bytes
              13 Dir(s)  11,361,357,824 bytes free
```

The output of the command shows us the drive letter C: and the directory name '\' (i.e. the 'root of C') and a list of files in that directory with their sizes and creation dates. <DIR> indicates that the entry is a directory (folder). The listing ends with a summary of the number of regular files, the number of directories and the amount of free disk space.

If we wanted to list the files of another directory or drive, we tell the DIR command this by means of an option consisting of the command, the option definition and the final carriage return. To see the files on the floppy in the floppy disk drive, for example, the command:

  DIR A: [CR]

will do the job. The 'A:' here is an option indicating the floppy disk drive.

If we want to display the output in wide format, then we use the switch '/W'.

SUGGESTED PRACTICAL EXERCISE

If you are looking at this material for the first time, you may well be confused by now! The best way to get a feel for the command line is to use one, so:

1 *Start a command line processor.*
2 *Issue the DIR command (don't forget the [CR]).*
3 *Try some variations on the DIR command like DIR /W and DIR /P.*
4 *Look up the Help for the DIR command by typing: DIR /?*
5 *Exit from the command line either by closing the window or by typing EXIT [CR] at your command prompt.*

The command set

Some of the DOS commands – like DIR – are common to all systems; others are specific to one or more versions of Windows. In order to explore the command set for your system, start a command prompt and type HELP [CR] – this will list the commands available on your system. You can then obtain detailed Help on the command by:

COMMAND NAME /?

COMMON COMMANDS AND HOW TO USE THEM

In order to do this exercise safely we will work with a floppy disk. We will also need to create a text file to use in the exercise.

> There's nothing particularly risky about the exercises in this chapter but it is good practice to avoid creating and deleting files on your hard drive. If you don't have a floppy drive you can use an alternative removable drive such as a USB stick in which case it will have a different drive letter.

1 *To create the text file, right-click on a blank area of your Desktop to get the context menu, and select* **New** *then* **Text Document** *as in the following figure. This will create a new text file.*
2 *Click the new Desktop icon to open an editor window. Enter some text like: 'This is a test' or 'Hello World' or anything else you like. When you have finished entering text, open the* **File** *menu, select* **Save** *to save the file, then close it.*
3 *Right-click on the new text file and rename it 'newfile'.*
4 *Put a blank floppy disk in the floppy disk drive.*
5 *Right-click on the newfile icon and select* **Send To Floppy Disk Drive (A:).** *This will copy the file to the floppy disk in the A: drive.*

	View	▶
	Sort by	▶
	Refresh	
	Paste	
	Paste shortcut	
	Undo Delete	Ctrl+Z
	New	▶
	Screen resolution	
	Gadgets	
	Personalize	

	Folder
	Shortcut
	Bitmap image
	Contact
	Journal Document
	OpenDocument Drawing
	OpenDocument Presentation
	OpenDocument Spreadsheet
	OpenDocument Text
	Rich Text Document
	Text Document
	Compressed (zipped) Folder
	Briefcase

6 *At the command prompt enter 'A: [CR]'. The prompt will now change to A:\> indicating that we are in the root directory of the A: drive.*

7 *From the A:\> prompt issue the command:*
   DIR [CR]
   This will show a directory listing and you will see newfile *which you copied earlier. At a command prompt level you can see the full name of the file and its extension,* newfile.txt.

8 *Floppy disks don't often contain subdirectories. But for purposes of the present exercise we will create one called 'test'. To do this, we use the MD (Make Directory) command from the A: prompt, like this:*
   MD test [CR]

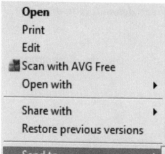

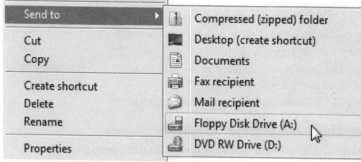

9 *We can now make this directory current by using the CD (Change Directory) command, like this:*
    CD test [CR]
10 *The prompt will now change to A:\test, indicating that we are in the test subdirectory. Issuing the command DIR at this prompt will show that the current directory contains no files.*
11 *To change back to the root directory of the drive use the command:*
    CD \ [CR]
12 *Now copy the file 'newfile.txt' to the test subdirectory by issuing the command:*
    COPY newfile.txt [SPACE] test [CR]
    You will see the message:
    1 file(s) copied
    Changing the directory to test and issuing the command DIR will show the new copy of the file in the test subdirectory.
13 *To delete the file, issue the command:*
    DEL newfile.txt [CR]

14 *To check that the file has indeed been deleted, issue the command:*
> DIR [CR]

15 *To go back to the root directory of A:, issue the command:*
> CD \ [CR]

16 *To remove the (empty) subdirectory test, issue the Remove Directory command:*
> RD test [CR]

17 *To take you back to the C: drive, issue the command:*
> C: [CR]

18 *From the C: prompt issue the command:*
> FORMAT A: [CR]
>
> *This will reformat the floppy disk, incidentally destroying all data on it.*

19 *Close your command prompt by typing:*
> EXIT [CR]

The practical exercise above provides an introduction to some important ideas: the hierarchical 'tree' of directories (folders) on a disk, the commands necessary to navigate between them, and how to create and remove both directories (folders) and files. Finally, you formatted your target floppy disk, thus removing all information on it and preparing it for further use as a clean disk.

The methods and commands used in the exercise can also be used to explore and work with similar structures on your hard disk. If you do this, do so with care. Never use destructive commands like DEL or FORMAT unless you are absolutely sure of what you are doing.

MORE COMMANDS AND HELP

There are many more commands available at the command line than we have seen here. The Help system will give you some insights into what they are and what they do. If you are interested in command line operations, by all means experiment further, but do so with care. Read the Help entries with care before trying anything – formatting your main hard drive (unless you mean to) is not generally recommended.

Batch files and CMD scripts

Any command which you type at a prompt may be put in a text
file and given the file extension .BAT (a batch file) or the extension
.CMD (a CMD script). Batch files use the older command processor
COMMAND.COM for backward compatibility with older DOS/
Windows versions. CMD scripts use the CMD.EXE command
line processor. Thus a file *myfile.bat* will run under the old
COMMAND.COM, whereas *myfile.cmd* would run under the
newer CMD.EXE. The system chooses the appropriate command
line processor on the basis of the file extension.

To create a CMD file of your own, you need to use a text editor
which outputs plain (ASCII) text. An ideal editor for this is
EDIT.COM. If you want to have a go at writing a CMD script –
admittedly a script that doesn't really do much – try this:

1 *Open a command prompt in a window.*
2 *Issue the command:*
    EDIT demo.cmd [CR]
    This creates the file demo.cmd and opens it for editing.
3 *In the newly opened EDIT window, type in the lines as shown
   in the screenshot:*

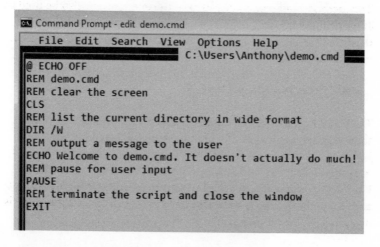

```
Command Prompt - edit demo.cmd
   File  Edit  Search  View  Options  Help
                              C:\Users\Anthony\demo.cmd
@ ECHO OFF
REM demo.cmd
REM clear the screen
CLS
REM list the current directory in wide format
DIR /W
REM output a message to the user
ECHO Welcome to demo.cmd. It doesn't actually do much!
REM pause for user input
PAUSE
REM terminate the script and close the window
EXIT
```

4 *When you have finished adding text as shown in the figure, save the file by opening the* **File** *menu, and clicking* **Save**.

5 *Having saved your file, click* **File** *again and this time, click* **Exit**. *This will return you to a command prompt.*

6 *To run your CMD file, simply type its name – in this case DEMO – at the command prompt. Note that you don't need to type in the CMD file extension for it to work.*

7 *If your DEMO file doesn't work as it should, make a note of any error messages, reopen the file with the command:*
   EDIT DEMO.CMD
(yes, you do need the file extension for this), edit your script, save it, close the editor window and run it again from the command line prompt.

HOW DEMO.CMD WORKS

The first line of our cmd file is @ECHO OFF. This means that the file will not output anything to the screen unless we specifically tell it to do so by using an ECHO command.

The second line begins with a REM statement. This is a comment or REMark, i.e. it's there to tell you, or anyone else who is reading the script, what it does: in this case it merely states that the name of the file is DEMO.CMD.

The third line is also a comment which tells us that the next line clears the screen.

The ECHO Welcome to ... causes the system to output the message shown.

The PAUSE statement causes the system to wait and to output a message 'Press any key to continue' until such time as a key is pressed.

The EXIT line causes the script to terminate and closes the window as soon as the user presses any key.

If you are interested in this aspect of your PC you will need to look at some professionally written scripts. If you use the Search utility in Windows – search on *.CMD – you will find a number of scripts on your system. By all means open them with an editor and look at them, maybe even print them off, but don't modify them – they may be important system components.

THINGS TO REMEMBER

1 *When you are working with CMD scripts you must use a plain text editor, NOT a word processor (unless it has a plain text mode).*

2 *Windows provides the EDIT editor which is ideal, but you can use any other programmer's editor instead.*

3 *REMarks in a CMD file are there for human readers; the system ignores them.*

4 *You can look at (but not safely alter) the professionally written CMD files on your system.*

6

Backup strategies

In this chapter you will learn:
* *about the types of backup*
* *how to organize rotating disk sets and archives*
* *how to backup CMOS and BIOS settings*

Backups

All versions of Windows have some form of Backup utility
built into them and these were the subject of part of Chapter 2.
However, the Backup utilities that ship with the various Windows
versions do not meet everyone's needs. Neither does making the
occasional – or even regular – backup of your files amount to a
backup strategy.

WHY BACK UP?

Just about everything on your system can be replaced: the
applications and programs, even the operating system itself can
be reinstalled from their original media (these are the main topics
of Chapters 12 and 13). What you cannot replace – unless you
have previously backed it up – is your own user data: your letters,
photos, essays, the chapters of the book you are writing.

The key to a successful backup strategy is to use the media and
methods suited to your needs in a systematic way.

A backup is just a copy of files and/or settings which have been copied to either a removable medium such as disk or tape, or to another independent system. In the event of a problem with the system, it can be fixed and the lost data restored from the backup copies. It is good practice to store backups away from the PC to which they relate (ideally in another building) so that, in the event of theft, fire, or other accident, the backup copy is safe.

There are many choices of storage media, including:

- *Writable CD/DVD disks*
- *Tape drives*
- *Removable disk drives – typically hard disk drives which connect through one of the USB or FireWire ports*
- *Pen drives (not recommended for long-term storage)*
- *Backing up to another system over a network or even the Internet.*

Writable CDs/DVDs

One of the easiest and most popular storage media for use in home systems is the writable – or rewritable – CD or DVD. CDs typically hold up to 650 Mb of data and single-sided DVDs have a capacity of 4.7 Gb. For many users a single disk may be enough to hold all their data.

In order to back up your files, you can use the **Send To** option from the context menu. Alternatively, you can click on **Computer** in the **Start** menu and simply drag and drop the files that you want to back up onto the CD/DVD drive icon. Whichever method you use you will be prompted to supply an writeable disk. If this is the first use of a new disk you will be prompted to choose how to use it.

As you can see from the figure you can use the disk 'Like a USB flash drive' or 'With a CD player'. The flash drive option is less portable, requiring Windows XP or later to read it. The CD player option is portable across many platforms. Any machine that can

read a CD can read your disk – ideal if you want to read your files on a different machine, even one that uses a different operating system such as Linux or a Macintosh machine with its MACOS X.

If your files take up more than the capacity of a single writeable disk you can, of course, choose the **Send to Compressed (zipped) Folder**, then save the compressed file to the burner drive. Although this may not be quite as portable as plain files, most systems can unzip a Windows compressed folder.

Tape drives

There are a variety of tape drives available. They are usually fitted in a spare drive bay on the machine in much the same way as a CD or DVD drive. Tapes are a slow, but high-capacity, storage medium, commonly used for overnight backup jobs of large server machines. Most home users won't need the capacity of a tape drive, but if you are one of the few that do, then have a look at Chapter 8.

Removable disk drives

These tend to be expensive, but can be very useful, especially if you have a lot of data. Usually, they are standard EIDE/ATA hard disk drives in one of the standard capacities – 80, 120, 500 Gb or more – housed in an outer case. They have their own external power supply, and the data connection is through either USB or FireWire.

To use a drive of this type, connect its power and data cables and turn on the power. After a few seconds, Windows will detect the new drive and assign it a drive letter. Once this has happened you can drag, drop, copy or delete just as you would with any other drive on your PC. When you are finished, the drive can be disconnected and stored away from the PC.

Pen drives

These are USB devices which will Plug and Play when you put them into a USB port. Windows detects them, assigns a drive letter, and they can then be used like any other drive on your PC.

Pen drives – sometimes known as 'gizmo sticks' – vary in capacity from 128Mb to 16Gb or more. Because of their small size, they are ideal for moving data between machines or as a short-term backup of files. Because USB is a cross-platform technology, these drives can be read/written to by other systems such as Mac or Linux-based machines. For all their advantages – small size, portability, relatively high storage capacity, these drives are a form of memory – flash memory – and may not be as robust for longer-term storage as other media.

BACKING UP OVER A NETWORK

If you have more than one PC, you may find it useful to back up data across your network. This can be done manually by copying files using drag and drop, or you may like to write yourself a CMD script to do the job. (Hint: look at the Help for the XCOPY command and experiment with that.)

Another possibility is to back up to an Internet Server. If you have your own web space you may be able to do this by uploading files to your own storage area using the File Transfer Protocol (FTP). Rather easier, perhaps, is to rent off-site storage with a service such as DropBox, which provides access to secure storage for a monthly fee. (DropBox offer a small amount of free storage in the hope that you'll buy more when you find out how useful it is!)

Backup types

DISK CLONING

The ultimate backup is a complete image of your hard drive: data, settings, installed applications, the lot. The best known software tool for doing this is Norton Ghost from Symantec.

Cloning a drive consists of making a byte-by-byte copy of the drive's contents and storing it in a single file which can then be restored in the event of problems. If, for example, you 'cloned' your current system by making an image in a file called *myimage.gho* this would, in effect, be a snapshot of your drive which you could store on a disk drive or a spanned set of CDs. Then, if your current hard disk fails, you can fit a new one and restore your system from your saved image.

This type of restore has the advantage of restoring everything – settings, saved passwords, the lot. However you can only restore what you backed up, so if you have deleted unwanted applications or data, they too, will be restored and anything newly installed since the cloning will not be present. Disk cloning can be very useful, but it is no substitute for a systematic backup strategy.

DISK IMAGING WITH WINDOWS

Since the introduction of Windows Vista, Windows has incorporated a disk imaging facility of its own that works as a cloning tool, though without some of the advanced features of third-party products. Chapter 2 looked at imaging and repair disks in Windows 7.

FULL BACKUP

As the name suggests this consists of backing up the whole of your system. This is a large undertaking and will require a lot of removable storage space such as a large removable hard disk. It is a job which needs to be done from time to time whether by running a backup program or by cloning the whole drive.

DIFFERENTIAL BACKUP

A differential backup copies all files that have been changed since the last full backup. It does not mark the file as being backed up, so it will be backed up again each time you perform a differential backup. If, say, you do a full backup on Monday and a differential backup on Tuesday and Wednesday, then files modified on Tuesday will also be included in the Wednesday backup even though they have been included in Tuesday's. If you have to restore your data on Thursday you will have to use the last full backup and the latest (Wednesday's) differential backup to recover all your data. Contrast this with the incremental backup.

INCREMENTAL BACKUP

An incremental backup backs up only those files which have been modified since the last backup of any kind. If you do a full backup on Monday and incremental backups on Tuesday and Wednesday, a file modified on Tuesday will not be included in the incremental backups made on Wednesday. If you have to restore your data on Thursday, you will need to use your full backup, then each of your incremental backups, in date order, to restore all your files.

Incremental backups are more economical of time and storage space and may be useful when backing up a large server, usually

	Full	Differential	Incremental
Monday	Includes all files	N/A	N/A
Tuesday	N/A	Backs up files modified on Tuesday	Backs up files modified on Tuesday
Wednesday	N/A	Backs up files modified on Tuesday and Wednesday	Backs up only files modified on Wednesday

using an automated system. For most of us, a combination of full and differential backups are probably the easiest to manage.

ROTATING SETS

It is usually advisable to have more than one backup for the simple reason that if the backup media are lost or destroyed, then restoring from an earlier backup is better than nothing.

There are a number of systems for rotating sets of backups – full backups and their associated incremental and differential sets – generally in some variant of grandfather, father, son. These arrangements are frequently used in business and commerce, and can be adapted to make a straightforward system which meets the needs of most home users. You will need two, or three, rewritable CDs or DVDs. Label them Disk 1, Disk 2 and Disk 3.

Start by backing up your user files to Disk 1. The easiest way to do this is to use the burning facilities included with Windows (see Writable CDs/DVDs, above). Put a label on the disk cover and record the date of the backup. Put it somewhere safe.

Decide how often you are going to back up – once a week may be enough, or you may want to back up every day – but whatever it is, stick to it. When the second backup is due, write your files to Disk 2, label and date it. When the third backup is due, do the same things with Disk 3.

When your fourth backup is due, erase the contents of Disk 1, burn your backup to the newly erased disk, label it and store it. Ideally, all your backup disks should be stored away from the system, in another room or even in another building. Every month or so, burn a permanent archive disk, label and date it, and store it well away from the system. This may also be a good time to create a system restore point as outlined in Chapter 2.

These arrangements are not 100% foolproof, but they are easy to operate and you can reasonably expect to recover most of your data in the event of a failure.

CMOS/BIOS settings

When you first turn your computer on it doesn't even know that it has an operating system. A chip, somewhere on the motherboard, runs some start-up routines – a basic memory check, detecting hard disk drives, etc. before it loads Windows (or any other operating system for that matter). This chip is known as the BIOS chip – Basic Input Output System.

When the system boots, the BIOS chip runs its built-in programs to set up the system, using information which is held in a small area of a special memory type called CMOS – Complementary Metal Oxide Semiconductor. The information in this CMOS memory is kept alive when the PC is turned off by a small battery, also mounted on the motherboard.

The CMOS battery – which looks like an oversized watch battery around the size of a £1 coin – is recharged while the PC is running and is discharged slowly when the machine is turned off. A flat or dead CMOS battery can cause the system to lose track of the time of day or even to fail to recognize some of its drives.

Replacing a defective CMOS battery is simple. Power down the machine, remove the case or cover, remove the old battery and fit the new one (see Chapter 7).

When you restart the machine after changing the battery, it may have lost some of its CMOS settings, so it is as well to know what these should be and how to restore them.

Windows does not give you the facilities to backup CMOS settings to a disk, so if you want to do this you will need to use one of the many third-party utilities that are available – searching the Web with the terms 'cmos backup utility' will lead you to plenty of them, some of them free.

However, it is really quite simple to access the BIOS/CMOS settings on your machine and write down the key settings with pen and paper.

HOW TO ACCESS THE CMOS/BIOS SETTINGS

Start – or restart – your PC. In the first few seconds you will see some text on screen – white on black, usually – which tells you the name of the BIOS manufacturer and the date that the BIOS was made. There is nearly always a screen message telling you which key to press to enter the Setup Utility – 'Press DEL to enter SETUP' is probably the most common of these, though other keys are sometimes used.

The first time you try this, you may find that the information shoots off the top of the screen before you have time to read it. If this happens, just press [Control], [Alt] and [Delete] all at the same time to restart the PC, and then try again.

When you have found and pressed the right key (or occasionally a key combination such as [Control] + [F2]) you will enter the setup program. Different manufacturers have different user interfaces and often different names for functions, especially for advanced features. However, the basic features are pretty standard.

- ▶ *Save and Exit*
- ▶ *Exit without Saving*
- ▶ *Standard Features*
- ▶ *Advanced Features.*

The first two options are important when you are working with CMOS/BIOS settings. If you change some settings, you want to save them so that the system remembers them for next time. Equally, if you get yourself in a mess (easily done!) Exit (or Quit) without saving will leave the previous settings unchanged.

The Standard Features option will generally list things like Time, Date, Sizes of Disks and Floppy drives. The Advanced Features will list things like Virus Warning (Enabled/Disabled), First Boot Device, Second Boot Device and so on. Make a note of these settings and store them somewhere safe. You may need them in the event of a flat battery.

While you are in the CMOS setup screen, why not take a look around at all those other options that you'll 'never need to use'? Providing you remember to Exit/Quit Without Saving you can do no harm to your system.

THINGS TO REMEMBER

1 *A backup method is not a backup strategy. You need a system to suit your needs – above all, you need to use it regularly.*

2 *CDs/DVDs that are used USB style are not portable across all platforms.*

3 *USB sticks are portable but not very durable.*

4 *You can use compression to create zip files that take up less space on your backup disks.*

5 *Don't forget to backup and/or make a note of your CMOS/ BIOS settings.*

6 *Like checking the tyre pressures on the car or defrosting the fridge, backing up data should be a regular household task.*

7

Inside the box

In this chapter you will learn:
- *how to work safely with hardware*
- *how to identify the main components*
- *why some things may not be worth upgrading (or replacing)*

Working safely

Modern hardware is generally robust and reliable, though occasionally a component may need to be replaced or upgraded. You may also want to add a component such as a sound card or a LAN card. This chapter and the next introduce you to the main components inside the case and how to work with them. Chapter 8 looks at the tasks of replacing these components in greater detail.

When working with hardware you are unlikely to harm yourself or your equipment providing you follow a few simple guidelines.

The most basic of these is: always power down and disconnect from the mains power source before you remove any covers or lids. PCs run on AC mains power – they are no more (or less) dangerous than any other mains-powered household gadget.

Once the machine is disconnected from the power, you will need to remove the lid, cover, or side panel in order to access the inside of the machine. Covers and panels are usually secured by two or three screws with a 'star' style head. The best tool for removing them is a Phillips #2 screwdriver. (Occasionally, usually on older systems, you may still encounter torxx screws. In this case you will need to use a torxx driver.)

Having removed the screws, put them somewhere safe: an ashtray or something of the sort is ideal. Next, slide back and remove the lid, cover, or side panel of the machine. If you haven't done this before, the inside of the system probably looks quite formidable. Don't panic – it's not half as complicated as it looks!

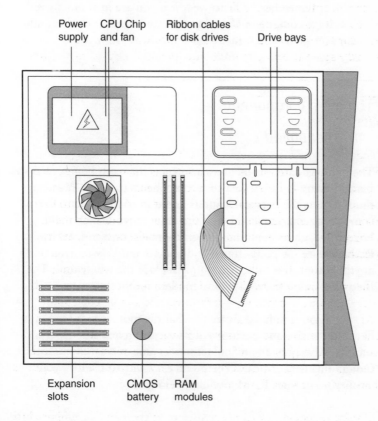

Power supply | CPU Chip and fan | Ribbon cables for disk drives | Drive bays

Expansion slots | CMOS battery | RAM modules

Before you touch any of the internal components, you should touch a bare metal section of the chassis of the machine. This safely discharges any static in your body – or at least equalizes it with any in the machine – so there is no difference of potential between you and the machine. Having discharged any static in this way, you should always touch bare metal before touching any component. Remember, even though you can't see static it can damage your system.

Wearing a wrist strap which you attach to the chassis of the PC means that you are permanently 'touching' bare metal. If you want a wrist strap, you can buy one for a few pounds from a local PC shop. Just remember NOT to wear it if you are in contact with high voltage equipment like a laser printer where it could conduct a high voltage to you rather than static away from you.

The main components

MOTHERBOARD

The motherboard – sometimes known as the main board, or system board – literally holds the other components together. You can think of it as the communications highway of the system. Every component communicates with the other components on the board through its communications channels, or buses. Like most PC hardware it's pretty tough and you are unlikely to need to do anything to it. If it fails, you simply replace the whole unit. The following figure shows a typical modern motherboard.

At this stage, simply be aware of what the motherboard looks like and the size and positions of its various expansion slots and sockets. Also note any manufacturer's name and serial numbers, though this isn't critical. (There's an easy way to identify your motherboard – see RAM modules, below.)

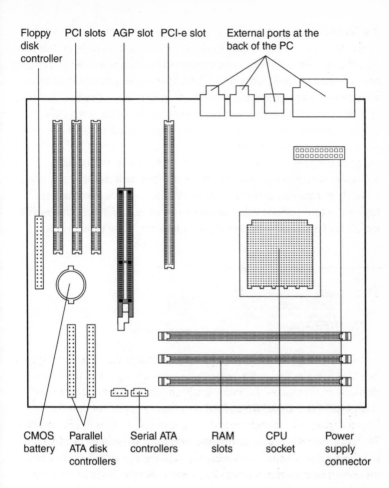

Floppy disk controller — PCI slots — AGP slot — PCI-e slot — External ports at the back of the PC

CMOS battery — Parallel ATA disk controllers — Serial ATA controllers — RAM slots — CPU socket — Power supply connector

CPU

The CPU – Central Processing Unit – is often thought of as being the 'brain' of the system, and sits in a socket on the motherboard. Because of the heat generated when it is running, it is fitted with a heat sink and a cooling fan. If the heat sink becomes clogged with dust or the fan doesn't work, your PC will overheat and stop working within a couple of minutes of being turned on.

RAM MODULES

These modules make up the main memory of the system. If you have one or more spare RAM slots on the board, then the most cost-effective upgrade you can do will be to add some more RAM. Most PCs bought from High Street or online retailers ship with enough RAM to work, but can usually be improved by adding some more.

Because the major manufacturers of RAM are in the business of selling as much of the stuff as they can, they will make it as easy as possible for you to identify your system and its memory needs. The following figure shows the results from a free utility downloadable from crucial.com. Note that it also identifies your motherboard.

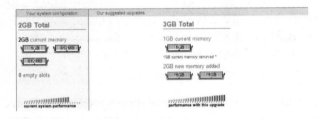

DISK DRIVE CONTROLLERS

The standard disk drive controller is the EIDE interface – also known as the parallel ATA interface. There are usually two of these on most motherboards. Each one has two rows of 20 pins and the surround to the pins usually has a slot so that the data cable which connects it to the drive can only be fitted one way. The cables themselves are usually round in section these days, but an older one may be a traditional ribbon cable. Ribbon cables have a red or pink stripe down one side – this indicates line 1. Where there are two controllers they are designated Primary and Secondary. Each controller supports two attached devices such as hard drives or CD/DVDs which are designated as either Master or Slave. Sometimes a primary controller is coloured red, blue or green to indicate that it is a higher speed type. This is not, however, an official standard and colours are often inconsistent.

Some newer systems may use Serial ATA (SATA) disk drives. The controllers for these are small rectangular connectors with just seven pins. It is possible to use a mix of SATA and parallel ATA drives, but it can lead to complications and is probably best avoided.

POWER SUPPLY UNIT

The Power Supply Unit (PSU) converts alternating current (AC) mains power to direct current (DC) which the PC can use. The highest output voltage from the PSU is 12 volts, so nothing 'downstream' of it is likely to do you any harm. The unit itself, however, carries full mains power and should be treated with caution. A PSU is an example of what the trade calls a 'field replaceable module'. In other words, if it fails, replace it as a unit – don't try to open it and fix it – bin it and fit another one!

The outputs of the PSU are to one of three standard connectors. There is a small connector for floppy disk drives (a Berg connector), a Molex connector for other drives such as hard disks, CD-ROMs, etc., and SATA connectors for Serial ATA drives. Of these three power connector types, the Molex is the commonest. It is a general-purpose power connector and can be used to supply power to anything from disk drives to fans. Where a device doesn't have the appropriate connector there is usually an adaptor cable available, for example, you can attach a Serial ATA drive to a Molex connector by using a SATA to Molex adaptor cable. You can also buy splitter and extension cables to increase the number of available power supply connections.

DISK DRIVES

Hard disk drives are usually 40-pin parallel ATA devices or, on newer systems, there may be 7-pin Serial ATA devices. The following figure shows a Serial ATA disk and connectors.

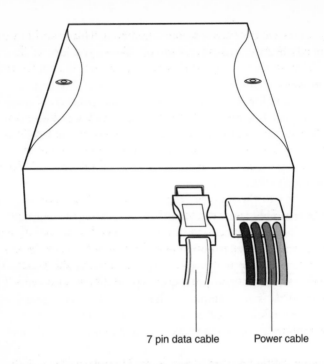

7 pin data cable   Power cable

Whichever type your system uses, it will need to be attached to an appropriate power line and a data cable. Power connectors are designed so that they will only fit one way and data cables are usually keyed so that they too, will only fit one way. Some older 40-pin cables may not be keyed, and the rule here is 'pink next to the power'. That is, the red or pink stripe down one side of the ribbon cable which indicates line 1 should be attached to the drive so that it is closest to the power connector.

CD and DVD drives – whether they are read only (ROM) drives or burners – are known collectively as optical drives because they work on laser light instead of the magnetic fields used by hard and floppy disk types. Even the fastest of these are relatively slow compared with magnetic hard drives, so they are frequently attached to the secondary EIDE/ATA controller, especially where this is the slower of the two controllers on the board.

Floppy drives are not fitted on some modern machines and this can occasionally be inconvenient. Chapter 8, shows you how to fit a floppy drive, so now is a good time to inspect your system to see if this is possible.

The first thing to check is that the case has a mount point for the drive. This will probably be a metal cradle about 3½ inches (9 cm) wide near the front of the case and on the outside you will see a blanking plate which is more or less the size of a floppy disk drive.

The next thing to check is the floppy disk controller on the motherboard. There is normally only one of these. At first sight it looks very like one of the hard disk controllers, but is smaller, with only 34 pins. As with hard disk controllers, it will usually be keyed so that it can only be connected one way and where this is not the case, there will be a red or pink stripe on the ribbon cable which indicates line 1.

GRAPHICS

Most modern systems use the Accelerated Graphics Port (AGP) or a card in the later PCI-e slot to output information to the screen. An AGP card is normally fitted in a dedicated slot on the motherboard, brown in colour, and not aligned with the other expansion slots. These vary in size and orientation according to the type of AGP card on your system. The PCI-e slot (more below) is a general purpose slot which is frequently used for graphics cards but may also be used for other purposes such as gigabit Ethernet.

Many systems, especially budget systems from High Street or online retailers, have on-board graphics – that is, a dedicated graphics chip connected directly to the motherboard. Most on-board graphics set-ups are suitable for relatively undemanding everyday applications like word processing, e-mail and browsing the Web. Sophisticated high-end games, or Computer Aided Design (CAD) packages may need a high-end graphics card in either an AGP or PCI-e expansion slot.

PCI EXPANSION CARDS

Peripheral Component Interconnect (PCI) is the standard for most expansion cards on modern systems. The PCI slots on your motherboard are white (or off-white) and there are usually three or four of them. Any PCI card can be fitted in any PCI slot and – given the right drivers – will Plug and Play 'out of the box'.

A newer standard PCI-e (the 'e' is for 'Express') provides a means of connecting faster PCI-e expansion cards to your system. The PCI-e slot is normally the same colour as the standard PCI slots and is physically longer. There are also four different specifications with different sized slots. Smaller (i.e. lower-powered) cards will generally work in larger slots but the reverse is not the case even where a card physically fits in the slot. PCI-e is increasingly used as an alternative to the Accelerated Graphics Port (AGP) for graphics output, though it can be used to attach other card types such as high-speed LAN adapters.

CMOS BATTERY

This is a small battery – like an oversized watch battery in appearance – which provides power to the CMOS while the system is turned off. In Chapter 6 we looked at the CMOS/BIOS settings. These settings are kept live when the PC is turned off because the battery provides the necessary power. Rather like the battery on a car, it is recharged when the system is running and discharges when the system is turned off. Repeated charging and discharging will eventually cause the battery to fail. When this happens, a common symptom is that the PC loses track of the correct time. If this happens, then it's time to replace the CMOS battery. These can be bought for a couple of pounds from electronics or electrical goods shops. They are more or less standard components, but an easy way to make sure that you get the right thing is to power down the machine, remove the old battery and take it to the shop and ask for 'another of these'. When you return with your new battery, put it in the holder on the motherboard, replace the case cover on the PC and reboot it. As the machine reboots, press the key to enter the CMOS Setup screen (usually [Delete]) and check that your system has correctly identified the disk drives, etc. You can reset the time and date here as well, but it may be easier to leave time and date settings and correct them through the Control Panel later.

Why some things aren't worth upgrading

PCs become more powerful and cheaper with every year that passes, and each release of the operating system and other software requires more and better resources. For the first couple of years of your PC's life you can probably keep up with this – a couple of sticks of extra RAM will improve the performance of your PC from day one. You can add to the total RAM count without throwing anything away.

If your hard disk is starting to get full, you can probably fit a second disk to increase you total storage – again, adding capacity without throwing anything away. However, the case for upgrading other components, such as the CPU, is not so clear cut. Suppose, for example, you were to buy a new CPU chip that was (say) 20% faster than your existing chip.

▶ *Is the chip compatible with other components on your system, especially the motherboard? Check with the motherboard manual and/or the manufacturer's website.*
▶ *Will the 20% faster chip result in a 20% increase in the overall performance of the system? The answer here is almost certainly 'No'.*
▶ *What do you do with the component you are replacing? Sell it? Throw it away?*

In general, you need to ask yourself whether in a world of ever-decreasing hardware and system prices, an upgrade is worth the effort and cost of doing it compared with replacing the computer.

Replacement, on the other hand, may well be cost-effective particularly on a relatively new machine where a component has failed. If, for example, your CPU chip has failed, you have no choice but to abandon the old one. The cost calculation here is simply whether it will be better to fit a new chip – possibly even a slightly faster one, a sort of 'incidental upgrade' – or abandon the old system altogether and buy a new one. The decision is more to do with finance than technology as such.

THINGS TO REMEMBER

1 *Always power down and disconnect before opening the case or removing any covers.*

2 *Always discharge any static in your body by touching bare metal on the case before touching any components. Better still, use an anti-static wrist strap.*

3 *Don't use a wrist strap when working with high voltage equipment such as laser printers.*

4 *Some components become hot during normal operation. Handle them with care.*

5 *PCI slots are universal – any PCI device will fit in any slot.*

6 *PCI-e slots come in various lengths and not all devices are compatible with all slots of this type.*

7 *Increasing the RAM installed on your system is a very cost-effective upgrade, particularly if you have any empty RAM slots.*

8 *Not everything is worth upgrading, particularly if your system is more than a couple of years old.*

8

Replacing and upgrading
hardware

In this chapter you will learn:
- *how to organize your work space*
- *what tools you need*
- *how to replace or fit individual components*

Before you start

Hardware components fit together like children's building blocks.
Most components fit only in the slot or socket for which they are
designed and on modern systems they are usually keyed so that
they only fit one way round.

ORGANIZE YOUR WORK SPACE

Time spent on preparation is seldom wasted, so before you start
taking things to pieces consider both where and how you are going
to work. Clearly, if you are going to do a straightforward job such
as adding a stick or two of RAM you will need no more than space
to lay the PC on its side, remove the cover and add the RAM. If, on
the other hand, you are going to change the motherboard, you will
need plenty of space to work and to store the many components
that you'll have to remove from the system.

The ideal work space will have a large flat work surface such
as a table or bench with adequate lighting. A desk lamp which
can be pulled over the work area as needed can be useful, as is

a magnifying glass and a small torch for reading small print on components that are buried deep inside the case.

A pen and paper for writing down settings or the position of cables and connectors is pretty much essential for all but the smallest jobs. Some people also use a digital camera to photograph these things.

You will need a Phillips screwdriver – preferably a #2 size – but it is also helpful to have a flat-blade screwdriver, a pair of fine-nosed pliers and one or two small containers such as ashtrays or yoghurt pots for the temporary storage of screws, jumpers or other small parts. Larger parts can often be stored in the upturned lid of the PC. If you are fitting a new component, leave it in its anti-static packaging until you are ready to use it.

Unless you have a dedicated work area like a garage, make sure you allow enough time to do the job. If you are working on the kitchen table and your spouse or kids have to kick you out in order to cook a meal, it will add greatly to the complexity of doing the job. As a rule of thumb, estimate how long it will take you to do the job, then double it, then add an hour!

How to add RAM modules

Most PC systems are sold with enough RAM to work but will give better performance with additional modules. The first thing to check is that you have one or more spare slots available and to compare the total installed RAM with what is recommended for your operating system.

Table 8.1 Memory requirements for Windows 7

Version	Minimum	Recommended
32-bit	1 Gb	2 Gb (or more)
64-bit	2 Gb	4 Gb (or more)

The recommended figures are, in reality, the minimum you will need to obtain anything like reasonable performance, and if you are planning on running any memory-intensive applications like sound or video editing then doubling the recommended (or more) RAM will be a worthwhile investment.

Total installed RAM can be found by right-clicking on (**My**) **Computer** and looking at its **Properties**. The number of empty RAM slots can be determined by taking the lid or side panel off the system and having a look.

The easiest way to find what types of RAM are available for your system is to visit memory manufacturers' websites and look it up. Crucial – one of the big manufacturers – has a free download program which will detect the type and amount of installed RAM and recommend (and give you a price for) upgrade options.

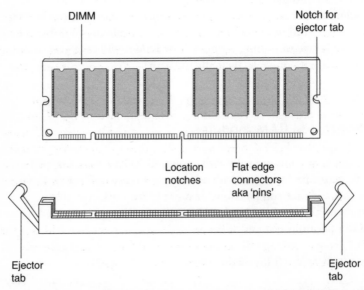

A typical Dual Inline Memory Module (DIMM). This type has notches in the face which fit into the motherboard slot so that it will only go in the right way around.

Having decided on the memory upgrade, and acquired it, you are ready to install. To fit the new RAM stick(s) you need access to the interior of the PC.

1 *Power down the PC, disconnect from the mains power supply, and remove the case, cover or side panel. Don't forget to touch bare metal or use a wrist strap before you touch any of the internal components.*
2 *If it is a tower case lay it on its side so that the motherboard is parallel to your work surface.*
3 *Remove the new RAM module from its packaging. Do not touch the connector edges with your fingers.*
4 *Flip back the ejector tabs on the motherboard RAM slot.*
5 *Check that the module is the right way round for the slot. (The notches on the underside ensure it will only fit one way.)*
6 *Push the module down into the slot, vertically, until the ejector tabs click into place, then push them gently to make sure that they are fully engaged.*
7 *To fit the module you will have to push it firmly into place, but you should not use excessive force. As with most hardware jobs, if you have to force it, you are probably doing it wrong – wrong orientation of the component with the slot or socket being the commonest error.*
8 *Repeat the steps for any other RAM modules. When you have finished, reconnect the power and start up the PC to check that the new memory is in place and working. All being well, the PC will beep once and boot to the operating system where you can verify that your new RAM is recognized by the system – right-clicking on (**My**) **Computer** will report the total installed memory.*

If the PC emits a series of beeps (not just a single beep, which is the PC's way of saying OK, at boot time) and fails to start properly, power down and reseat the memory and try again.

Once the RAM is in place and working, power down, replace the covers or panels which you removed in order to gain access, and power up again. Job done!

Replacing a power supply unit

The power supply unit in your PC takes alternating current from
the mains supply and converts it to 12 volt, 5 volt and 3.3 volt
direct current for use by the system internally. If a PSU simply dies
the PC won't work. If it is failing – delivering less than the required
voltage – you may experience boot time failures. In this situation
the PC will start to boot, then fail. Repeating the attempt may
secure a successful boot and the machine will run, but there will be
problems next boot time. To check the output of the power supply,
use a multimeter on its output lines. You should see readings of
12 volts (yellow), 5 volts (red), 3.3 volts (orange). As little as
one-tenth of a volt below the required voltage can be enough to
cause problems.

As is frequently the case, the easiest solution is to replace like with
like, though you may want to increase the wattage rating of the
new PSU if the old one is rated lower than (say) 400 watts.

To replace a PSU:

1 *Power down the PC, disconnect from the mains supply, and
   remove the case, cover or side panel.*
2 *Disconnect the power lines from the various drives and the
   motherboard.*
3 *Turn the PC so that you are looking at the back of the
   case.*
4 *Remove the screws (usually four) which hold the PSU in
   place.*
5 *Remove the old PSU.*
6 *Put the new PSU in place and fix it with the screws you saved
   from the old unit.*
7 *Connect output lines to the motherboard and the
   drives.*
8 *Power up and test, then power down and replace the
   covers.*

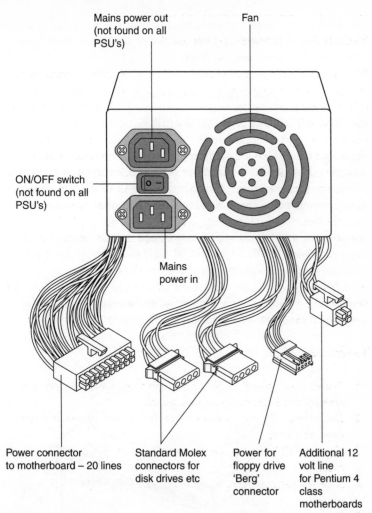

Mains power out
(not found on all
PSU's)

Fan

ON/OFF switch
(not found on all
PSU's)

Mains
power in

Power connector
to motherboard – 20 lines

Standard Molex
connectors for
disk drives etc

Power for
floppy drive
'Berg'
connector

Additional 12
volt line
for Pentium 4
class
motherboards

An ATX Power Supply Unit.

Note: the connector to the motherboard is keyed so that it will
only fit one way, and the Molex connectors (4 pins) have two
bevelled edges so that they can only be fitted the right way round in
the disk drives. Any drive can take its power from any connector of
the appropriate type.

Be careful, too, when reconnecting the floppy drive. It is possible, but difficult, to force the power connector on upside down, and doing this will burn out the drive.

How to add a second hard disk

Adding a second hard disk drive increases your storage capacity in a very cost-effective way. Your operating system and programs remain in place on your primary drive (the C: drive) and – after fitting – your new drive is available for additional storage.

Most PCs are equipped with a single hard disk drive which is either a serial or parallel ATA type. Serial ATA uses a small flat 7-pin data connector and a 15-pin power cable (see the figure on page 96).

Parallel ATA uses a 40-pin connector and an 80-line ribbon cable for data, and a standard Molex connector for power.

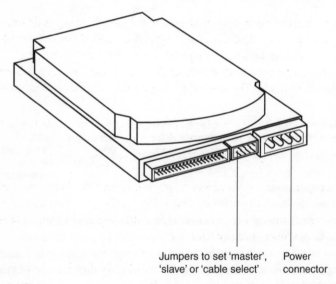

Jumpers to set 'master', 'slave' or 'cable select'   Power connector

A parallel ATA drive.

While it is possible to mix drive types on the same system it is best to use similar types. If your first drive is serial, use a serial drive for the second drive: if the primary is a parallel drive then use a parallel drive for the second drive.

MASTERS, SLAVES AND JUMPER SETTINGS

Unlike the more modern Serial ATA (SATA) drives, parallel ATA drives and CD/DVD drives, require you to set jumpers to identify the drive as 'master' or 'slave'.

Most motherboards have two 40-pin connectors for ATA drives (see Disk drive controllers, in Chapter 7) and each controller supports two devices referred to as master and slave. This is needed to distinguish the drives which are sharing a controller and a cable. To do this you set a jumper on the back (or sometimes the underside) of the drive. Jumper settings are usually indicated by a label on the drive. For each cable, set one drive as master and the other as slave using the jumpers.

An alternative to this method is to use the cable-select (CS) option. Systems which use cable-select have colour coded connectors on the data cable. To set up a pair of drives using this method, set the jumpers on both drives to the CS option and attach them to the data cable. The colour coding on the cable works like this:

▶ *Blue connects to the motherboard*
▶ *Grey connects to the slave drive*
▶ *Black connects to the master drive.*

By convention, the Windows operating system is usually on the master drive on the primary controller (drive C:) – this was a requirement in earlier versions of Windows and has remained as a (rather sensible) convention.

Regardless of the drive type, it will need to be fixed in the case and attached to both power and data cables.

Power down the PC, disconnect it from the mains and remove the cover or side panel to access the inside of the machine. Set jumpers, where necessary, fit the new drive in a spare bay and connect the power and data cables. Reconnect the machine to the power – don't put the lid or side panel back yet, you may have to adjust or correct something if you make a mistake. If you do get it wrong – it's quite easy to set a jumper incorrectly – the system won't work, but you won't do any damage. Just start again and experiment until you get it right. Something to watch out for, particularly with older drives, is different jumper settings for standalone master and master with slave present.

With your new drive in place, reboot the machine. If you have set the jumpers correctly and connected the data and power cables as required, Windows will find the new drive when you reboot.

The next job is to prepare it for use.

PARTITIONING AND FORMATTING A NEW HARD DISK

1 *Navigate to the Disk Management tool using* **Control Panel > System and Security > Administrative Tools > Create and format hard disk partitions.** *You will see something like this:*

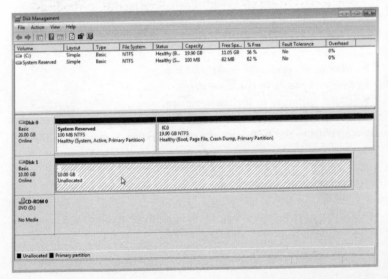

Note that the system is showing the size and status of all attached disks. The first entry shows the two partitions on the first hard disk (Disk o) which were created by Windows during the installation process. Don't even think about messing about with these!

2 The bottom entry, CDROM, tells us no more than that we have a DVD drive which currently has no disk in it. The entry which interests us at present is the new Disk 1. Right-click on the new disk (Disk 1) and select **New Simple Volume** *from the context menu.*

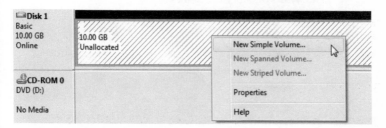

3 *This starts the New Simple Volume Wizard. Click on the* **Next** *button on the welcome screen. You will be asked to specify the*

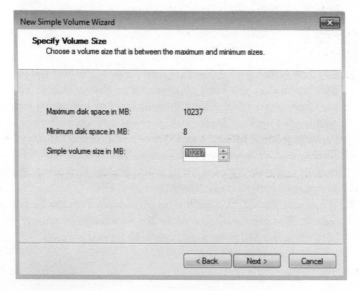

*size of the new volume. The default is to use the whole of the available disk space. Click on **Next** to accept this default.*

4 *At the next screen, set the drive letter for the new volume (accept the default unless you have reason to do otherwise) then click on **Next**.*

5 *You now have the option to change various aspects of the new volume before proceeding further.*

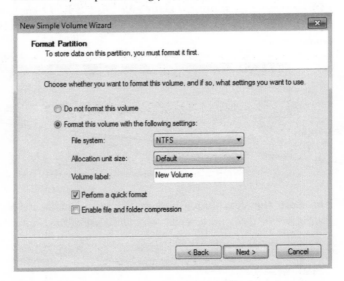

6 *The File system and Allocation unit defaults are best left as they are (unless you have good reason to change them). You may like to change the New Volume label to something more meaningful such as 'Data Disk' perhaps and uncheck the **Perform a quick format** box to force a full format. Make your choices and click on the **Next** button. The Wizard will now present you with a summary of your choices. You can go back and make changes if necessary.*

7 *When you are satisfied with your choices click on the **Finish** button. Windows will now make the necessary changes. If you have chosen a full format this can take several minutes – a tea-break's worth at least.*

On completion the system will show the new disk, its size, file system and the volume name that you chose.

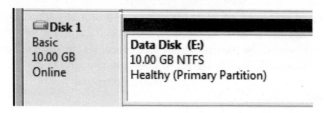

Right-clicking on the newly created volume provides further tools that you can use with your new disk.

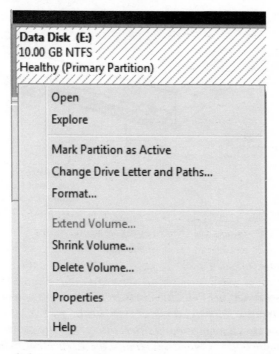

Your new disk is now ready to use. Power down, check that all cabling is neatly arranged and nothing is snagging, replace the cover or side panel, put the machine back in its proper place and turn it on. Finally, congratulate yourself on a job well done!

How to add or replace a CD or DVD drive

Adding or replacing a CD or DVD drive is a similar undertaking to fitting a second hard disk, but is easier to do because the new drive does not need to be partitioned or formatted. (Note: hard disks are ATA devices, CD/DVDs are ATAPI devices, though the distinction is not important for our present practical purposes.)

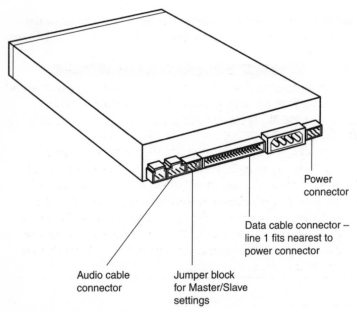

Power connector

Data cable connector – line 1 fits nearest to power connector

Audio cable connector

Jumper block for Master/Slave settings

The back of a typical CD/DVD drive.

1 *Power down the PC, disconnect from the mains power supply, and remove the case, cover or side panel.*
2 *If you are replacing an old drive, disconnect the cables from the back of the drive, remove the screws that hold it in place (usually two on each side) and slide it out of the front of the case. Note the position of the jumper which sets master or slave and use the same jumper setting on the new drive.*

3 *Slide the drive into place, attach cables as for the old drive.*
4 *Fix in place with the screws saved from the old drive.*
5 *Turn on and test before powering down again and replacing the cover or side panel.*

If, rather than replacing a CD or DVD drive, you are adding one, the procedure is fundamentally similar. The easiest way is to add the second drive to the spare connector on the data cable attached to the first. Having opened the PC case:

1 *Remove the cover from the drive bay on the front of the PC. You may also have to break out a small metal internal cover.*
2 *Check the jumper setting on the existing drive and set the jumper on the new drive to be the opposite (so that you end up with one master and one slave on the same cable).*

Adding a tape drive

Tape drives are most commonly used to back up server machines in the commercial world where there may be a lot of data which changes rapidly. Not many home users will need a tape drive, but if you are one of the few, then it's really much the same as fitting a CD/DVD drive. Choose a drive which uses the standard 40-pin ATA style connector, choose appropriate jumper settings as for a CD/DVD drive and fit it in the case.

How to fit a floppy drive

Many modern PCs are sold without a floppy drive which can be inconvenient for some maintenance jobs. There are external floppy drives available, but you can fit an internal one easily for a few pounds as long as you have a floppy controller on the motherboard and a 3½-inch bay on the front of the case. Fitting a floppy drive means that you will have a drive for running diagnostic programs or for copying small files to another PC.

The first thing to do is to check that you have a drive bay available and that there is a floppy controller on the motherboard. Remove the side panel or cover of the PC and check. The floppy controller on the motherboard has 34 pins in two rows and looks like a smaller version of the hard disk controllers.

You will need a floppy drive and a floppy drive cable. These are normally quite cheap to buy. They are also very easy to fit.

To fit your new floppy drive:

1 *Power down the PC, disconnect from the mains supply and remove the cover. The drive bay at the front of the case will have a plastic cover plate: this can be pushed out from behind. If there is a metal cover behind it then this too must be removed by breaking it. It is made of a soft alloy and is usually perforated to make it easy to break out. It may not feel right, but it is intended to be broken and removed.*
2 *Slide the new floppy drive into the bay, and line up the front of the drive with the front of the case. Inside the case, the drive will be sitting in a metal cage with fixing points on either side. There are usually two screw holes on each side of the drive itself. Fit the screws in the sides of the drive so that it is held in place. Don't overtighten them.*
3 *After you have double-checked that the drive is properly aligned with the front of the case, fit the data cable.*

A floppy cable has 34 connectors for the 34 pins on the drive. Cables and drives are usually keyed so that they can only be connected correctly. Where there isn't a keying system, the coloured stripe on the edge of the cable indicates line 1. Pin 1 on the drive is probably marked, though it is not always easy to see.

There is a twist in the cable between the end connectors. The last connector – the one after the twist – is the one you should connect to the floppy drive. This ensures that the new drive will appear on the system as Drive A:. (The other connector – the one before the twist – is for drive B: on a twin floppy machine.)

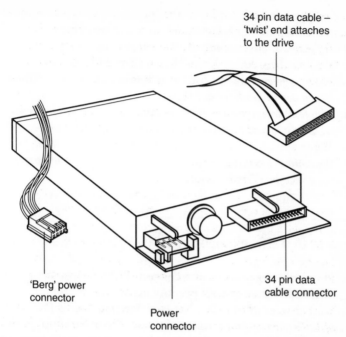

34 pin data cable – 'twist' end attaches to the drive

'Berg' power connector

Power connector

34 pin data cable connector

A floppy disk drive and data cable. There are two connectors fairly close to one another at the drive end of the cable (so that you can fit two floppy drives if you want to) – the other end of the cable fits on the motherboard.

4 Connect the other end of the data cable to the controller on the motherboard. Where the controller and the cable are keyed, the cable can only be fitted correctly, otherwise the coloured stripe on the cable should correspond with pin 1 on the controller.

5 Finally, fit the power connector to the floppy drive. There is really only one way that this will fit, but it is just about possible to force it on the wrong way. If you do this you will damage your new drive. The data cable is not so critical.

6 With the new drive in place, reconnect the PC and turn it on. Watch the light on the new floppy drive. If it has been fitted correctly the light will flash briefly as the system starts up, and then go out. If the drive light remains permanently on, then the data cable is fitted back to front (i.e. pin 1 on the drive is connected to line 34 on the cable). If this happens, you

won't have damaged the drive – power down and reverse the orientation of the cable on the drive and try again.

7 *If, at this stage, nothing at all is happening, it may be that the new drive has to be enabled in CMOS/BIOS. Refer to the* How to Access the BIOS/CMOS Settings *section of Chapter 6 if you are in doubt about this.*

8 *The final test, with the PC running, is to put a floppy disk in the drive and test that the system can read and write to it. When you are satisfied that all is well, power down the PC, disconnect from the mains and replace the cover/side panel, then reconnect and reboot.*

How to fit a PCI expansion card

The Peripheral Component Interconnect (PCI) expansion slot is the most widely used general purpose expansion slot for adding hardware devices to your PC. Network Interface Cards (NICs), internal modems, sound cards, additional USB or FireWire ports can all be added to your system through the PCI slots. A more modern variant of PCI is the PCI-X slot (PCI eXtended) – this is a higher speed development of the standard PCI slot and is a different length to the standard PCI connector.

Provided the expansion card and the slot match, the procedure for fitting a new PCI card is the same for all types and devices:

1 *Power down.*
2 *Fit the card.*
3 *Power up.*
4 *Install any necessary drivers.*
5 *Reboot the PC and test.*

Modern Windows versions support most of the common hardware expansion cards out of the box – that is, the operating system ships with the necessary software drivers. However, if there are drivers provided by the manufacturer with the card, these may be more up-to-date and you may wish to use these, or download the newest drivers from the manufacturer's website.

If you are going to use the manufacturer's own drivers, read the fitting/installation instructions first. Some devices require you to install drivers before fitting the expansion card.

If your device Plugs and Plays (and most devices these days do) then you can either choose the Have Disk option to install the manufacturer's drivers, or install the drivers provided by Windows with a view to updating them later.

To update drivers for a device, navigate to Device Manager, select the device in question, right-click and select Update Driver. This launches a Wizard which allows you to search both local drives and the Internet for drivers.

How to fit a PCI-e or AGP graphics card

Fitting a PCI-e or an AGP graphics card is much the same as fitting a standard PCI card. Check that the card is of the right size and type for the slot on your motherboard, power down, fit the card, power up and test.

By default – even without additional drivers – your new graphics card will give you some sort of output – usually a screen resolution of 800 × 600 – which is sufficient for you to install the full set of drivers for the card.

Your new card will be accompanied by a CD containing the manufacturer's drivers. Read the instructions, then install the drivers. Reboot the PC if necessary and configure your graphics settings. To do this, right-click on a blank area of the Desktop, select **Properties** and choose the **Settings** tab. Here you can set the screen resolution, number of colours, etc. You can also use the Advanced option to change other settings such as the monitor refresh rate. Be careful with this because although a rate that is too low can cause eye strain, setting it too high can permanently damage the monitor. (It is rare that a software setting can damage hardware, but this is the exception that proves the rule.)

How to replace a motherboard

Replacing a motherboard is probably the most ambitious hardware task that you are likely to tackle. To keep things simple, I shall assume that you are simply replacing like with like – i.e. the same make and model.

If you want to upgrade to a different motherboard, there are many considerations about compatibility with your other components, and you may well have to reinstall the operating system. This is of course possible, but is beyond the scope of this book. As it is, even replacing like with like is close to rebuilding the whole system.

Once you have identified your motherboard and bought the replacement you are ready to begin. Allow plenty of time for this and make sure that you have space to lay things out, containers for screws, pen and paper and, if possible, a digital camera.

1 *Begin by disconnecting the PC and removing the side panel. Take a close look at the layout of the internal components and make notes of the position of various cables – particularly the small cables that attach to the LEDs on the front of the case. A couple of photographs of the inside of the case will be very useful at this point. Take them and make sure that you can access them or print them for future reference.*
2 *There is no set order for removing the components from the case, though it's probably easier to remove the cables first. As each component is removed place it somewhere safe, away from the immediate work area.*
3 *Remove all of the expansion cards, but leave the CPU chip and RAM modules in place. Remove the fixing screws that*

hold the motherboard in place and lift it out. (This might be
a good time to clean out some of the dust!)

4   In the now empty case you will see some brass fixing points
for the motherboard. These are known as posts or standoffs.
Their purpose is to provide fixing points for the motherboard
which will hold it in place without touching the case.

5   Remove the new motherboard from its anti-static packaging
and put it in the case, lining it up with the standoffs. Make
sure that the external ports line up with the openings in the
back of the case. (A second pair of hands at this stage can be
very useful!) With everything lined up, screw the motherboard
to the standoffs, making sure that the screws are tight, but not
using excessive force.

With the new motherboard in place, it's time to check the job.
This is a two-stage process. We start with a 'bare bones build'.

1   Remove the heat sink and fan from the old processor.
The fan will unscrew, and the heat sink is normally held
in place by a clip. The CPU itself is held in place by a lever
which is part of the CPU socket. (This is known as a Zero
Insertion Force or ZIF socket and the lever as a ZIF lever.)
Pull the ZIF lever until it is vertical and remove the chip.
Put it in the ZIF socket on the new motherboard – it will
only fit one way. If the processor is properly oriented and
seated, the ZIF arm will drop down easily and fix the CPU
in place.

2   Fit the heat sink on the top of the newly installed CPU and fix
the fan. Make sure that the power lead to the fan is connected
to the motherboard and that it is the right way round.

3   Transfer the RAM modules to the new motherboard. Connect
the power supply to the motherboard and reconnect the small
wires from it to the front of the case. Make sure that the case
speaker is reconnected.

4   Now, in this half-assembled state, connect the system to the
mains power and turn it on. Make sure that the CPU fan
works as soon as the system is powered up and if it does not
switch off immediately and fix it.

5   Once you are sure that the CPU fan is working, allow the
    PC to go through the boot sequence. If the motherboard
    is properly installed and the CPU and RAM are correctly
    installed the machine will start to boot. The case speaker will
    emit a lot of rapid beeps – this is the machine complaining that
    it can't find its keyboard, disk drives, etc. This is good news –
    if it's whingeing it's working! You have a successful bare
    bones build. If it's not working, then there are only a handful
    of components to check – that's the point of the bare bones
    build – to keep things simple. It's easier to debug a handful of
    components than a whole system!

6   With the basic build in place and working, you can replace the
    disk drives and other components. With a graphics card and
    monitor in place you will get visual output. Replacing the hard
    drive will give you an operating system, and so on until you
    have a fully rebuilt working system.

7   When you have finished your rebuild, replace all covers
    and panels, reinstate the machine to its proper place in the
    household and test everything you can think of.

THINGS TO REMEMBER

1   *Organize your work space before you start.*

2   *Have all tools, installation instructions, driver CDs, etc.
    to hand.*

3   *Always power down before removing the panels/covers on
    the PC.*

4   *Always use anti-static precautions – preferably a wrist strap.*

5   *Where system memory – RAM – is concerned more is
    better – always!*

6   *A failing Power Supply will cause boot problems. Check
    with a multimeter because as little as a tenth of a volt below
    requirements can cause problems.*

7   *There are no user serviceable parts in a PSU – replace it and
    dispose of the old one in accordance with local laws/disposal
    guidelines.*

8   *Read the instructions twice, do the job once, and test the
    results before replacing the panels/covers on the PC.*

9

....

Preventive maintenance

In this chapter you will learn:
* *how to organize your maintenance schedule*
* *how to work without damaging your equipment*
* *how to dispose of old computers legally and safely*

A maintenance schedule

Preventive maintenance and cleaning are tedious but necessary if you want to keep your system running efficiently, and a regular maintenance schedule can save you time and money on maintenance and repair bills.

The key to effective maintenance is a regular pattern of work. Some tasks should be done daily, some weekly, some occasionally. Many routine tasks – such as backups and virus scans – can be automated through Windows.

Daily
▶ **Virus scan.** *Your virus scanner should have the capability of running at a pre-set time each day. If you leave your system permanently on, you can schedule this for the small hours of the morning. Don't forget that the scanner needs to update its 'definitions' files, so schedule the update to run just before the scan. There's more on viruses in Chapter 16.*

- ▶ **Spyware scan.** *This complements the virus scan and ideally, it should be done immediately before or after the virus scan. More in Chapter 16.*
- ▶ **Backup.** *It is prudent to back up your data daily. The minimum you should do is to back up data which has been modified (a differential backup) with a full data backup once a week. Chapter 6 has more on this.*

Weekly
- ▶ *Full data backup, preferably to a rotating disk (or tape) set.*
- ▶ *Defragment the hard disk (see Chapter 1).*
- ▶ *Run the Disk Cleanup Wizard (see Chapter 1).*

Monthly
- ▶ *Clean optical drives – CDROM/DVD – with a cleaner disk.*
- ▶ *Archive backup of data – store away from the PC.*
- ▶ *Mouse – if you are still using a 'ball' mouse, clean the rollers by scraping gently with a toothpick or similar.*
- ▶ *Monitor – power down and clean the screen with a soft cloth or an anti-static wipe.*
- ▶ *Check the keyboard for sticky keys – clean with canned air if necessary.*

On failure
- ▶ *Floppy disk drive. The cleaning disk which you can use for cleaning floppy drives is mildly abrasive, so it should only be used sparingly to avoid long-term cumulative damage to the drive.*

Yearly
- ▶ *Case. Open the case. Remove dust deposits by brushing gently with a natural bristle brush, then blow out with canned air, or use a special PC vacuum cleaner.*
- ▶ *Adaptor cards, cables and removable components – clean contacts and reseat.*

Ongoing/as required

▶ *CMOS – record and/or backup CMOS settings.*
▶ *System – maintain a record of hardware, software and settings of the system. Don't forget your e-mail account settings, dialup numbers and passwords. Note all changes in a system notebook – that's 'notebook' in the old fashioned sense of a pen and paper record – it doesn't need mains power, batteries, or disk storage and there's a lot to be said for that!*

Cleaning products and tools

Commonly used products and tools include:

▶ **Canned air**. *Use this for blowing dust from awkward corners. Most PC shops sell it.*
▶ **Natural fibre brushes**. *A small paint brush or a pastry brush is ideal. Make sure, though, that it has natural bristles as some man-made fibres can generate static electricity which could damage components.*
▶ **Antistatic wipes**. *These are usually individually wrapped. They can be bought from most PC shops.*
▶ **Denatured alcohol**. *This can simply be a bottle of meths or surgical spirit which you can buy from a hardware shop or pharmacy. Alcohol cuts through grease very effectively and evaporates quickly.*
▶ **Mild detergent solution**. *Tap water with a squirt of washing-up liquid is a very good cleaning solution, especially for the outside of the case, etc. It needs to be used with care, of course, as water and electricity can be a hazardous combination. Don't apply the solution directly, use a dampened cloth and use sparingly.*
▶ **Cleaning disks**. *The disks which you use on a floppy drive are mildly abrasive and should be used with restraint. The cleaning disks/kits which you can use for CD or DVD drives are not generally abrasive and can be used as necessary or monthly as a routine preventive measure.*

- **Cotton buds.** *These are useful for general purpose cleaning. They can be used in conjunction with canned air and a natural bristle brush for mechanical removal of dirt and debris from awkward corners. They can also be dipped in alcohol for liquid cleaning where necessary.*
- **Non-static vacuum cleaners.** *These are small cleaners – often pistol grip in shape – which are intended for use with PCs. They need to be used with care as there is the possibility of damaging or dislodging components.*

Before using any product on your PC, check that it is suitable for its intended use. For instance, if you plan on cleaning the case with a detergent solution or alcohol, apply it to a small area that is usually out of sight to check that it's okay.

In terms of Health and Safety law in the UK, there are regulations under the Control of Substances Hazardous to Health (COSHH) regulations, and in the USA all such products have a Material Safety Data Sheet (MSDS). You can check the nature of any product by searching on the Internet.

Cleaning

THE CASE

Power down and 'wash' with a cloth that has been dipped in mild detergent solution and wrung out. Allow the cleaned surfaces to dry fully before reconnecting the power. For a really good job, you can follow detergent cleaning with a rub down with a cloth that has been moistened with alcohol. Again, allow the cleaned surface to dry fully before reconnecting the power.

MONITORS

LCD – flat panel – monitors can be cleaned with a glass cleaner and a lint-free cloth. Don't spray the cleaner directly on to the screen, but apply a small amount to the cloth, then wipe the surface with it. LCD screens are easily scratched, so you should work gently. Be careful not to leave any excess on the screen and allow half an hour or so before powering up again.

Cathode ray tube (CRT) monitors – the ones that look like television sets – need to be treated with care. Even when they are turned off they contain very high voltages. Always disconnect the monitor before working on it and never wear a wrist strap or even metal jewellery that could come into contact with it.

A simple soap-and-water solution can be used for cleaning the outside of the case and the screen itself. Don't use excessive amounts of the solution: dip the cleaning cloth in it, then wring out until it is damp but has no excess moisture. Clean the monitor and dry it with a clean cloth before powering up. Don't use commercial cleaners or aerosol sprays other than those specifically designed for use with monitors.

With either type of monitor, power up when you have finished and the screen is dry, then check that any controls for brightness, alignment, etc. are okay. It's quite easy to knock a control accidentally during cleaning and to lose the 'picture' as a result.

INSIDE THE CASE

Dust is an ever present problem with computer systems. The components generate static charges as a by-product of their operation, and the various cooling fans draw air (and dust) into the case. Over time, the accumulation of dust can be sufficient to cause overheating, so an annual spring clean of the interior of the case can be a useful investment of your time.

As with all work on the inside of the system box, power down and disconnect from the mains before removing the covers or side panels.

The first line of defence against accumulated dust is a small paint brush, or a pastry brush, with natural bristles which will not induce static in the components to which it is applied. Simply use the brush to dislodge accumulated dust – particularly on the CPU heat sink/fan assembly and the power supply fan. The loosened dust can be blown away using canned air or removed with a non-static vacuum cleaner.

While you have the case open, it is a good time to check that all of the fans rotate freely and are properly connected to the power connectors on the motherboard – it's quite easy to dislodge connection during the cleaning process. This is also a good time to replace any missing covers from unused expansion slots. This will help to optimize the airflow in the case and to keep atmospheric dust out.

Before replacing the cover or side panel, connect the machine to the mains and power up. Check that all fans – particularly the CPU fan – are working. A non-functioning CPU fan will cause the chip to overheat and the system will lock up in under a minute. Longer than a minute is sufficient to cause permanent damage so this is a check worth making.

CONTACTS AND CONNECTIONS

This is not really necessary where a system is functioning properly, but some people like to clean and reseat internal components as part of their annual maintenance. If components have been handled and fitted properly – that is, contacts and edge connectors have never been touched by hand – then there is not likely to be any corrosion or oxidation to the surface.

If you do find it necessary to clean edge connectors on expansion cards or memory modules, then remove the module and use a very fine emery cloth or a specialist electrical contact cleaner spray. The easiest method is to use a pencil eraser to brush the contacts. When doing this, always work from the inner to the outer edge of the module to avoid peeling back the edge connectors.

Other internal components which fit into slots or sockets on the motherboard may work themselves loose over time. The repeated cycle of heating and cooling causes repeated expansions and contractions of the components which can cause them to work loose in their sockets – a phenomenon known as 'chip creep'. As a preventive measure, it may be prudent to remove and reseat any such components to establish a fresh electrical contact.

REMOVABLE MEDIA DEVICES

Removable drives such as tape drives, floppy drives, CDs, DVDs, etc. are open to the air, and the media themselves are physically handled. This means that they can collect dust and finger grease which can be transferred from the disk to the drive heads. An indirect form of preventive maintenance, then, is to exercise care when handling removable media.

Magnetic media, floppy disks and tapes, etc., can easily be corrupted if they are stored close to strong magnetic fields, so you should avoid storing them near anything with an electric motor – like a vacuum cleaner – or anything with strong electro-magnetic fields such as CRT monitors or speakers.

When it comes to cleaning drives themselves, there are two approaches: removal and manual cleaning or using cleaning tapes or disks. Generally speaking, floppy drives are now so cheap that it may be cost-effective to replace then rather than spend time on cleaning them, though cleaning kits are available.

Optical drives – CD and DVD – as well as tape drives may be removed, stripped down and cleaned with alcohol and a lint-free cloth. A cotton bud dipped in meths is an easy way to clean a lens. As an alternative, there are cleaning disks and kits available for most drive types. Optical media are mechanically 'swept' clean by brush heads mounted on a cleaning disk which passes over the laser lens. This is a non-destructive process. Cleaners for magnetic media are generally mildly abrasive so, whilst they are effective at removing the build up of contaminants on the drive heads, excessive use can shorten the life of the drive.

VENTILATION, DUST AND MOISTURE CONTROL

Fortunately, PCs do best in the same sort of conditions that most of us find comfortable: not too hot, not too cold, moderate humidity and no sources of dust. Most domestic users will have no problems, but air conditioning systems can sometimes lower humidity to sub-optimal levels.

When you are carrying out preventive maintenance inside the case, look out for unusual patterns in the (inevitable) build up of dust in the case as these may indicate missing expansion slot covers or cracks in the case.

Safety

SURGE SUPPRESSORS

Mains electrical supplies are subject to interruptions, voltage 'sags' and occasional 'spikes'. In commerce and industry, key machines are often protected by various technologies such as line conditioners and uninterruptible power supplies. For most home users, these technologies are disproportionate and expensive. However, a simple surge suppressor costs only a few pounds and will provide basic protection against power surges in the mains supply which could otherwise damage your system. If you don't have a surge suppressor – buy one!

SAFE DISPOSAL OF OLD EQUIPMENT

Nearly everything inside a computer seems to be toxic and there are increasing levels of concern by government and local authorities about safe disposal. Before disposing of any piece of equipment it is wise to enquire about current legal requirements for the country, county or state where you live.

Batteries contain many toxic substances and need to be disposed of through a recognized disposal facility. They should never be incinerated or thrown out with household rubbish. Batteries which are damaged, or which leak, present a hazard to anyone handling them – be especially careful not to get electrolyte in your eyes.

Monitors – particularly CRT monitors – contain many toxic substances and may contain potentially lethal voltages even when they have been turned off for some time. They are subject to ever-tightening disposal regulations and you should find a specialist disposal facility.

Toner cartridges, refill kits and old ink jet cartridges may also need special disposal. However, many of these items are refillable and/or recyclable. Empty laser toner cartridges may even be saleable.

If you are in any doubt about the nature of any component or substance that you have to dispose of, then a search of the Internet for the UK Control of Substances Hazardous to Health (COSHH) regulations or the US counterpart Material Safety Data Sheet (MSDS) will give an indication of what is appropriate and/or legally required.

THINGS TO REMEMBER

1 *Routine maintenance may be tedious to do, but it really does keep your system running better for longer and will save you money.*

2 *Many routine tasks – such as backups and virus scans – can be automated through Windows.*

3 *Check any substance that you intend to use on a small area of the PC that is normally out of sight.*

4 *Don't clean a floppy drive unless it needs it. The cleaner is mildly abrasive and can damage the drive over time.*

5 *CD/DVD drives can be cleaned regularly because the cleaner disks are not abrasive.*

6 *You can use a drinking straw in place of canned air in an emergency. Just blow gently though the straw and be very careful of introducing moisture to the component.*

7 *Always power down before cleaning the PC case or components with liquid cleaners.*

8 *Be especially cautious when cleaning a CRT monitor – even when disconnected, they contain very high voltages.*

9 *Check the environment where you are using the PC – dust and excessive humidity are both potential sources of long-term damage to your system.*

10

....

Peripheral devices

In this chapter you will learn:
- *about the main external ports*
- *about the cables and connectors associated with each port*
- *how to install device drivers*

_____

Ports

From the earliest days of the PC, systems have been built to be
extensible by attaching additional components to the expansion
slots inside the case and attaching peripheral devices – printers,
scanners, cameras, etc. – to the PC's external ports.

Ports are integrated into the system through their connection
to the motherboard. This may be an attachment through an
expansion card in a slot, or it may be an 'on-board' port, that is,
directly connected to or built into the motherboard at the time of
manufacture.

Whether they are on-board or on expansion cards, the main PC
ports provide a means of connecting external – or peripheral
devices. Some of them have only one purpose – dedicated ports
such as VGA or DVI for graphics output – or they may be general-
purpose ports which allow the connection of any device which has
the appropriate interface.

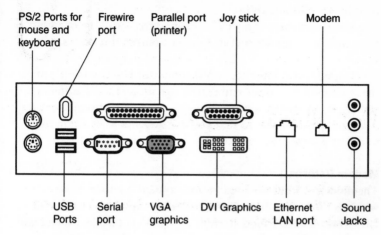

PS/2 Ports for mouse and keyboard | Firewire port | Parallel port (printer) | Joy stick | Modem

USB Ports | Serial port | VGA graphics | DVI Graphics | Ethernet LAN port | Sound Jacks

The common ports that you might expect to see at the back of a PC.

Some of these ports – particularly USB and FireWire – are often fitted to the front of the case on modern PCs. There are even instances of USB ports built into the side of a Flat Panel monitor. However, their location does not dictate their use.

DEDICATED PORTS

Keyboard and mouse (PS/2s)
The small round connectors for the keyboard and mouse are known as PS/2s after the IBM PC model of that name. More often that not, these days, they are colour coded: purple for the keyboard and green for the mouse. This is not an official standard – just a convention that has emerged in recent years. If your connectors are not colour coded there will usually be some indication on the case of which is which. You need to exercise care when reconnecting these. If you plug the keyboard into the mouse port (and vice versa) and attempt to reboot the PC you won't do any damage, but you may find that it will refuse to start up at all. If you do get this wrong, power down before putting it right. PS/2 connectors are not 'hot swappable'.

Graphics – VGA and DVI

The Video Graphics Array (VGA) connector is still the one most frequently used for a monitor. It has 15 pins in three rows.

The Digital Video Interface (DVI) connector has 29 pins: 24 of these are used for power and digital signals, and five for analog signals. It is sometimes referred to as a '24+5 DVI Connector'. Adaptors are available so that you can attach a VGA connector to a DVI port and vice versa.

Modem (internal)

The modem port at the back of your system is known as an RJ11 which is the United States' standard telephone connector. In the UK, you will need a modem cable with an RJ11 at the PC end and a standard BT connector at the other. If the cable has RJ11s at both ends, you can use an adaptor at the phone end.

Configuring a modem – whether internal or external – may require you to provide software drivers. You will also need to enter some information from your Internet Service Provider (ISP) such as the dialup phone number, your user name and password. Installing and configuring a modem is a topic in Chapter 15.

Network: RJ45

The RJ45 is similar in appearance to the RJ11 though it is slightly larger. It is the most commonly used network connector. It may be built into the motherboard or it may have been added through an expansion card.

If you have installed a new Network Interface Card (NIC) or have reinstalled Windows you may have to provide drivers for it. Most hardware of this type will Plug and Play – just follow the instructions on the screen. If it doesn't Plug and Play run the Add New Hardware Wizard which you can access through the Control Panel.

Configuring the network connection – IP addressing, etc. – is covered in Chapter 17.

INSTALLING A MONITOR

Attaching a monitor is really as simple as plugging it into the graphics port, providing it with power and booting the PC. If it is a new monitor, Windows will detect it at boot time and you may be prompted for drivers from the manufacturer's CD.

Once the drivers are installed you may need to tweak a few settings. There are usually some controls – buttons, most likely – on the front of the monitor which can be used to change the position of the picture, its height, brightness, contrast and so on. These controls will be specific to your monitor so you should consult the manual or instructions which came with it. Failing that, just sit and experiment, making notes if necessary, until you obtain the display characteristics you want.

Having set the monitor to your liking through hardware, you may want to further fine-tune it through the operating system. Navigate to **Control Panel > Appearance and Personalization > Adjust Screen Resolution**. You will see something like this:

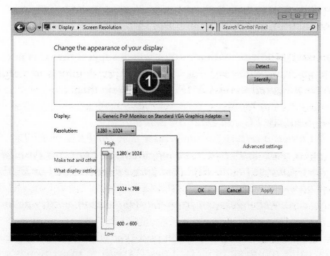

Experiment until you find resolution and colour quality settings which suit you. LCD (Flat Panel) monitors are generally designed to work at one optimal resolution. CRT monitors are more flexible in this respect. If you click **Advanced** and select the **Monitor** tab you can change the refresh rate of the monitor. This is the frequency with which it redraws the lines which make up the display. If it is set too low it can cause eyestrain; if it is set too high you can damage the monitor. Most people find a refresh rate in the range 75 Hz to 85 Hz comfortable to work with.

PARALLEL PORTS

The parallel port has been a part of every PC from the very earliest days. It is 'D' shaped in section and has 25 pins and data lines. Originally it only allowed data to pass in one direction: from the PC to the attached device. Since it was mainly used for attaching a printer to the PC it is often referred to as a printer port or PRN or LPT1.

Modern systems are more demanding than the early PCs. These days we expect a printer to be able to send back error or status messages such as 'out of paper', or to be able to run diagnostics or print-head cleaning and alignment utilities. We may also want to connect a device such as a scanner where the data flow is predominantly to (rather than from) the PC.

If you have problems with a printer which suggest that it is not communicating with the PC it may be that the printer port needs to be reconfigured in the CMOS Setup. To do this:

1   *Reboot the PC and enter the Setup utility.*
2   *If there is a setting for the printer port (or PRN or LPT1) and it reads SPP then it is configured as a Standard Parallel Port. Change this to EPP (Enhanced Parallel Port) or ECP (Enhanced Capabilities Port).*
3   *Save your changes, exit from the setup screen and try again.*

Note that the highest specification port type (ECP) may require a special cable to use all of its facilities. As with so many things with a PC, experiment until you find something that works for you. (There's more about CMOS/BIOS settings in Chapter 6.)

SERIAL PORTS

Serial ports have also been part of the PC since the earliest days. By modern standards, they are slow, but they are still sometimes used. Like the parallel port they are 'D' shaped in section. Unlike the parallel port they are invariably male. The commonest size for a serial port is nine pins, though the older 25-pin version is still sometimes used. Serial ports are also referred to as RS-232 ports since their functionality is defined by the Recommended Standard 232 of the Electronic Industries Alliance (EIA) – an American Standards body.

Serial cables have 9-pin or 25-pin female connectors at each end corresponding to the pins on the ports. A standard serial cable is 'straight through' – that is, pin 1 at one end connects to pin 1 at the other, pin 2 to pin 2, and so on. However, there is a variant which is used for transferring data between two PCs on a direct back-to-back connection where some of the lines are crossed over so that the send pin at one end corresponds with the receive pin at the other. These crossover cables are known as null modem cables and can be difficult to distinguish from standard ones.

The standard serial ports and (to a lesser extent) parallel ports are rapidly being superseded by the newer high-speed general purpose ports: USB and FireWire/IEEE 1394.

USB

As personal computing developed, particularly in terms of multimedia devices, the limitations of the older serial ports became all too apparent. In terms of speed and usability, the traditional port did not meet users' needs for fast hassle-free connection of devices such as cameras, external disk drives, etc.

The Universal Serial Bus (USB) was introduced in order to meet the demand for a high-speed port which would allow for the connection of different peripheral devices. The current standard is USB 2. USB is a continually developing technology under the control of the trade association. Details are available from their website at www.usb.org.

USB 2 supports three speeds of operation: 1.5Mbps for slow devices such as mice and keyboards, 12Mbps for fast devices (the original speed of USB 1) and 480Mbps which is known as Hi-speed. Most modern systems support the Hi-speed USB 2, but if you have the older USB port, newer devices can still be attached though they will only operate at the lower (USB 1) speed.

USB 3

This is the latest version of USB and is also known as SuperSpeed USB

USB 3 consumer products are becoming available (from 2010) so this is not yet a widely supported technology. It offers higher data transfer rates but requires its own special cable type to achieve them. It is plug compatible with older USB ports. At the time of writing (March 2010) USB 3 drivers are 'under development' for Windows 7 but are not actually available yet, so for most of us this is a technology to watch rather than to implement.

One of the major advantages of USB is that it allows 'hot swapping' of components. In order to connect a USB device you simply plug it in to any USB port and the system will sense the change in voltage on the interface, query the device, assign it an identity and load any necessary drivers.

Installing a new USB device needs to be approached with care. Read the installation instructions carefully, preferably twice. In general, most USB devices require you to install drivers before connecting the device. Some may then require a second level of driver installation after connecting. This is not as complicated as it may sound: it's just a matter of doing things in the right order. Chapter 15 covers connecting a USB broadband modem.

There are two standard USB connectors, Type A and Type B. The Type A connector is flat and rectangular in section and the Type B is almost square. The Type A connector is usually at the PC end of the connection with the (smaller) Type B at the device end. There are also 'mini' connectors which are used mainly with small devices such as cameras.

Using one or more USB hubs means that you can connect more devices than you have physical ports on the PC. Typically, you connect a Type A connector at the PC end and a hub at the device end. The hub provides additional Type A ports which can be used to connect other devices (including hubs). In theory, USB can support up to 127 devices simultaneously.

Unlike the older port types, USB is often implemented as a front-of-case port. This makes it easier for the user to take advantage of its hot swapping capabilities.

Low-power devices, such as mice or keyboards, can draw power directly from the host PC (up to 0.5 amps of power per port) but this is obviously unsuitable for power-hungry devices such as printers. These need their own external power supply.

When buying a new USB device be sure to check its power requirements and intended speed of operation. If you have to attach a high-speed device to a legacy (USB 1) port it will usually work, but only at a fraction of the USB 2 speed. If you are stuck with USB 1 ports (unlikely on a modern machine) you can add USB 2 ports through a PCI expansion card.

The Institute of Electrical and Electronic Engineers (IEEE) standard IEEE 1394 defines a standard for a high-speed serial connection which is the main rival to USB. The name FireWire is often applied to all devices conforming to this standard but it is in fact a brand name of Apple Computing Inc. Other brand names which conform to the IEEE 1394 standard include: i.Link (Sony) and Lynx (Texas Instruments). The IEEE 1394 specification is sometimes known as 'Serial SCSI'. Like USB, IEEE 1394 is a continually developing standard. The Trade Association website is www.1394ta.org and this is the best source of up-to-date information.

The IEEE 1394 connector is bigger than USB with two bevelled edges at the top of the connector so that it can only be connected the right way round. The standard connector has six pins, two of which are for power. There is also a four-pin variant for devices which have their own power supply. This can cause problems when connecting multiple devices in a chain. If you connect a six-pin device 'downstream' of a four-pin device it cannot receive power because there is a break in the power connection to the PC. The answer to this problem is to connect the devices in a different order or to use an external power supply.

Whilst they are different technologies, USB and IEEE 1394 are rivals in the market for high-speed, hot-swappable, easy-to-use connections. At the time of writing the main differences between them is that IEEE 1394 is faster (and usually more expensive) and it supports isochronous data transfers (i.e. real-time transfers) which make it particularly suitable for transferring audio and video data at the same time. For this reason, it is often the technology of choice for data transfers from – or between – movie cameras. Where the cameras – or other devices – support it, IEEE 1394 can manage transfers of data between devices without being attached to a host PC.

All modern Windows versions support IEEE 1394, just as they do USB. If your PC doesn't have IEEE 1394 ports they can be added through a PCI expansion card. There are even cards which provide a mixture of IEEE 1394 and USB ports.

Device drivers

A device driver is a piece of software that enables a hardware component to communicate with the rest of the PC. Drivers may be supplied with the Windows Operating System, on a disk – usually a CD – included in the manufacturer's packaging of the device, or downloaded from the manufacturer's website.

INSTALLING DEVICE DRIVERS

Many common devices, such as the more popular network cards (internal devices) or printers (external or peripheral) devices are supported by Windows 'out of the box'. That is to say, when Windows 'discovers' a new device it will look for a suitable driver and if there is one, will install it with the minimum of user intervention.

The drivers which are supplied with Windows are probably adequate for the job. They may even be the best drivers for the job, but there is no guarantee of this. Technology moves quickly and the drivers that were shipped with Windows may have been superseded by newer ones.

Where a device has manufacturer's drivers – usually supplied on a CD and packaged with the retail product – these may offer enhanced capabilities or better performance that the ones supplied with Windows. The older your Windows version, the more likely this is to be the case.

A third possibility, is that the manufacturer has updated the drivers for the device since it was assembled and packed and made available for retail sales (possibly several months before) and that the latest and best drivers can be downloaded from their website.

Whatever the source of your device drivers, check the product and its documentation before using them as there are different approaches to installing them on your system.

The most straightforward case is the device which Plugs and Plays and then prompts for drivers. Providing the drivers are bundled with the operating system or you have them on CD all you need to do is to follow the instructions on the screen. You may well have to reboot the system in order to complete the process, but it is essentially a straightforward one.

Some devices, however – particularly USB devices – require you to install drivers before adding or attaching the hardware. If you don't do this you will probably end up with a device that doesn't work – or doesn't work properly. If this happens, cut your losses, uninstall the drivers (navigate to Control Panel > Programs > Uninstall a program) and start again. As someone once said: 'When all else fails, try reading the instructions!'

Occasionally, you may come across a device which has a two-stage process for driver installation: install drivers, attach device, install further drivers – usually with a reboot somewhere in the sequence of events.

Elsewhere in the book, there are worked examples of installing device drivers which illustrate these points:

- ▶ *Adding a network interface card – Chapter 17*
- ▶ *Installing a printer and setting up a share – Chapter 11*
- ▶ *Installing a USB broadband modem – Chapter 15.*

SIGNED DRIVERS

When installing device drivers you may receive a warning from Windows that the driver is 'unsigned' – this is usually nothing to worry about.

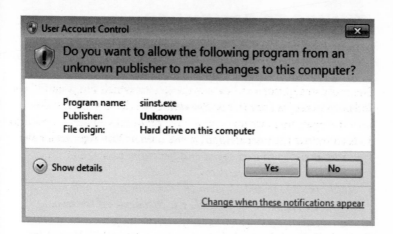

Microsoft have a scheme whereby manufacturers can submit a driver for testing and, providing it meets the necessary criteria it may be approved by Microsoft as being compatible with their Windows operating system – this is a 'signed' driver.

For various reasons, manufacturers do not necessarily follow these procedures for the 'signing' of their products and there are even installation instructions supplied with a device which tell you to ignore the warning and proceed anyway.

THINGS TO REMEMBER

1 *Keyboard and mouse connectors are not hot swappable. If you need to change them, power down first.*

2 *All USB devices are hot swappable.*

3 *High-speed USB devices will work with earlier versions of the port but with reduced speed and functionality.*

4 *Network (RJ45) and Modem (RJ11) connectors and ports are similar in appearance. The RJ45 is the larger of the two.*

5 *A parallel port is also known as a Printer Port, PRN, or LPT 1.*

6 *FireWire is a brand name that is often loosely used to indicate all IEEE 1394 devices.*

7 *'Unsigned drivers' are probably safe to use provided they came from a reputable source such as the manufacturer's CD that came with the device or the manufacturer's website.*

11

Printers

In this chapter you will learn:
- *about common printer types*
- *how to connect a printer and install drivers*
- *how to share a printer on a network*
- *what to do if your printer doesn't work*

Printers are peripheral devices which attach to one of the standard ports on the PC, so it may be useful to refer back to Chapter 10, as background information for this topic.

Printers usually attach to the parallel port on the PC (which is why it is frequently referred to as 'the printer port') or increasingly nowadays to one of the USB ports. Very occasionally you may encounter a 'serial printer' which attaches to the older style 9-pin or 25-pin serial port.

Of all the devices which you may want to attach to your PC, a printer is probably the most complex and most likely to have non-standard features. Whereas the PC is based on some well-known industry standards, printers are considerably more diverse in what they do and how they do it. For example, most printers have some sort of test routines built into them. You may, for instance, be able to print a test page from a printer which isn't connected to a PC by holding down a particular combination of function keys on the printer as it powers up. However, the precise nature of the test and the key combination needed to access it will vary from printer to printer. The standard advice to read the manual first is especially important when working with a printer.

Common printer types

The main printer types in use today are:

▶ *Ink jet (and bubble jet)*
▶ *Laser*
▶ *Multi-function (usually based on an ink jet or laser jet).*

There are other printer types for specialized work – photographic, dye sublimation, thermal, wax jet, and so on. These are not normally used by home or even small office users, so we will concentrate on the main types only.

INK JET/BUBBLE JET

Ink jet and bubble jet printers (known collectively as ink dispersion printers) are very popular with home and micro-business users. They are slightly more expensive to run than laser printers in terms of consumables – ink/toner – but they are reasonably priced and can produce full colour output which varies in quality between draft and photographic. Using specialized papers can further increase the quality of the finished printed output.

Ink jets form an image by squirting very small dots of ink on to the paper. The print quality is measured by the number of these dots per inch and may range from 150 dots per inch (DPI) to 1400 (and higher).

Ink jet printer speeds are rated in pages per minute (rather than characters per second) because the ink jet doesn't form each character separately, it prints a line across the page which contains only a portion of the image whether character or graphic. Most inkjets print bi-directionally and produce 2–9 pages per minute (PPM).

The paper feed mechanism on ink jets may be single sheet manual feed but is usually a cut-sheet feeder. The paper is fed past the print head by a series of rollers that hold it in place. It is advanced one print line at a time. The finished page is stacked face up.

There are various arrangements for supplying ink. Usually there is a reservoir of black ink and a combined red/blue/yellow reservoir, though increasingly these days the coloured inks each have a separate reservoir.

Some printers have the print head built into the reservoir so that the electronics are replaced every time the ink is renewed; other printers have the print head built in so that only the ink and its container are replaced. There is a price/reliability trade-off here and this may be one of the considerations when evaluating a potential printer.

Common problems with ink jet printers

The main problem encountered with ink jet and bubble jet printers is the tendency for the ink to dry and clog the nozzles. To counter this all ink jet printers move the print head to a special position known variously as the park, cleaning or maintenance area.

Most ink jet and bubble printers have some sort of head cleaning or diagnostic mode built into them which is accessed by holding down some combination of keys. This is probably specific to the make or model of printer so you should consult the manual for your printer. There is also software support for cleaning and aligning print heads as a supplement to the printer drivers on the manufacturer's disk for many printer models. If you can't find such a utility on your driver disk it may be worth visiting the printer manufacturer's website to see if such a utility (possibly as part of an updated driver package) may be available.

LASER PRINTERS

The laser printer is pretty much the standard choice for business users because of its lower running costs and quality of print finish. A print from an ink jet, for example, will 'run' if it becomes wet, whereas the laser process produces a very stable finish.

In recent years, laser printers have become more reasonably priced – a black-only laser desktop printer can be bought for well under £100 – so laser printers are now an option for some home users.

The laser printing process is similar to the working of a photocopier. It uses a fine dust of toner to create the required image on paper and this is fused on to the finished print by passing it through a heated roller known as a 'fuser'. This accounts for the slightly 'cooked' feel of a printout when it emerges from the printer.

The heat involved in the laser printing process also means that you need to be careful when printing onto transparencies for overhead projectors. Make sure that you are using transparencies that are intended for use in laser printers. If you use anything else – transparencies which are intended for an ink jet or hand writing – they will melt as they pass through the printer and it will be severely damaged – probably to the point of being a complete write-off.

Maintenance tasks with laser printers

Apart from general cleaning – removal of dust and paper debris, etc. – there is little to go wrong with the mechanism of a laser printer that can be serviced by the user. You will need to replace the toner when it runs out, of course, and on many laser printers this consists of dropping in a complete unit which means that many of the components which are sensitive to everyday wear and tear are replaced as a matter of course.

Many of the more expensive laser printers – such as the Hewlett Packard LaserJet series – can be refurbished from maintenance kits which provide replacements for components which are known to be prone to wear and failure on that particular model.

Common problems with laser printers

Probably the most common cause of poor quality prints from a laser printer is the wrong type of paper or other printing surface. If there are problems with print quality, the first thing to check is the paper.

Break open a new packet of standard photocopy paper and try printing on that. If this cures the problem then your printer is okay, but your print surface is not. This can be the result of using the wrong type of surface – too smooth or too rough at the microscopic level – or inappropriate storage conditions for your paper stock.

If inappropriate print surfaces have been ruled out then you may have a hardware problem. Most laser printers have some form of diagnostic self-test mode and this is useful if only to establish whether the problem encountered is in the printer itself or in the PC which is the source of the print job.

If you have problems, try the following:

▶ *Replace the toner cartridge*
▶ *Check cabling*
▶ *Replace the data cable*
▶ *Turn off any advanced functions.*

If none of these work it is probably not a user serviceable problem. For an expensive professional office printer, you may be able to take it to a registered service centre. For the cheaper models the best solution may be replacement.

MULTI-FUNCTION PRINTERS/SCANNERS

There has been a massive growth in the popularity of multi-function printers in recent years. These are usually based on ink jet technology, but they offer a range of features over and above simple printing.

Typically, a multi-function printer will also be a scanner, photo-copier and fax machine and may well have a slot where you can insert the memory card from a digital camera and print your photographs directly from it.

Multi-function printers vary considerably in their details between makes and models so it is especially important to consult any documentation or manuals provided with the product that are specific to it.

Whatever the details of your particular make and model, there are some general maintenance guidelines. In addition to checking the quality and condition of the paper, cable connections, ink levels, and running head cleaning routines, you may need to clean the inside of the printer.

1 *Disconnect the printer from the mains supply*
2 *Remove any covers or access panels*
3 *Remove any dust, dirt or debris from the interior*
4 *Clean internal parts with a dry cotton swab or lint-free cloth*
5 *Remove any stubborn deposits by dipping the swab or cloth in a very small amount of water or denatured alcohol*
6 *Make sure that everything is clean and dry before replacing covers, powering up and testing.*

After doing these maintenance tasks you may have to recalibrate the printer/scanner. You will need to follow the detailed instructions in the manufacturer's manual to do this.

Printer connection methods

CONNECTING TO THE PARALLEL PORT

The commonest way of connecting a printer to a PC is through the parallel port on the back of the machine. A standard parallel printer cable has a 25-pin male end which attaches to the port on the back of the PC and a Centronics connector which attaches to the printer. (These are very distinctive in appearance and can only fit one way.) Connect the printer to the PC with the printer cable and turn it on. Unless it is something very unusual, Windows will detect it and it will Plug and Play. You may have to provide drivers as part of the installation process. We will look properly at installation shortly.

CONNECTING TO A USB PORT

Connecting a printer to a USB port is similar to using the parallel port. The USB cable will have a Type A end – flat and rectangular in section and a smaller Type B connector which goes at the printer end. Even if you have front USB ports, it is probably as well to connect the printer to one of the ports at the back of the machine and save your front ports for equipment such as cameras or flash memory sticks where you may want to use the hot swap capabilities of USB.

Connect the Type B connector to the printer and power it up. Do not connect to the PC until you have read the installation instructions that came with the printer. Many USB printers require you to install drivers before connecting to the PC and if you don't do this you will probably end up with a printer that is 'installed' but which won't actually work.

With the necessary drivers installed, plug the Type A connector to the port on the PC and turn the printer on. Follow the instructions on screen to complete the installation process – see also the next section.

Installing a printer

WINDOWS PLUG AND PLAY

Windows 7 Plug and Play supports most commonly used printers so before you try anything else simply connect and power up the printer and see what happens. With luck you will see something like this:

A minute or so later you will see a message: 'Your device is ready to use'.

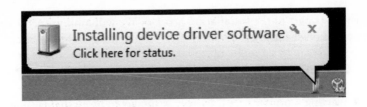

Installing device driver software

Click here for status.

MANUAL INSTALLATION

This example walks through the process of installing an Epson photo 890 to the parallel port of a Windows 7 PC. There may be minor differences when installing other makes of printer but this should still serve as a generic guide to the process.

Before you start, make sure that you have any manufacturer's CD to hand along with documentation, cables and connectors. Unpack the printer and read any instructions that come with it – twice!

Click on **Devices and Printers** in the **Start** menu (it's a short-cut to the appropriate Control Panel entry) – you will see all currently connected printers and devices. To start the process of installing the new printer click on the **Add a printer** button (near the top of the window). Note that USB printers are Plug and Play. However, in this example we will be installing a parallel port printer on the default parallel printer port LPT1.

1 *Click on the Add a Local Printer option.*
2 *Accept the default option to install to LPT1 by clicking on* **Next**. *This will take you to the window shown in the following figure:*

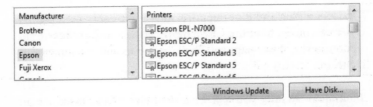

Manufacturer	Printers
Brother	Epson EPL-N7000
Canon	Epson ESC/P Standard 2
Epson	Epson ESC/P Standard 3
Fuji Xerox	Epson ESC/P Standard 5
	Epson ESC/P Standard 6

Windows Update   Have Disk...

3 *You have two choices:* **Windows Update** *or* **Have Disk.** *If you have a fairly popular printer from a major manufacturer the Windows Update option may well do the job. However, for purposes of this example we will examine the Have Disk option.*

4 *Click on the* **Have disk** *button. You will be prompted to provide the driver disk. When the CD is inserted it should autorun and present you with something like this:*

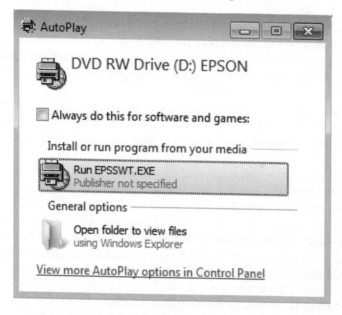

5 *Click on the Run option. You will see an Unsigned Drivers warning. Click on the* **Yes** *button to proceed.*

In the unlikely event of the installer disk not auto-running you can navigate to the CD drive through the **Computer** entry in the **Start** menu and look for a file called 'setup.exe' – clicking on this will start the installer.

6 *The set-up program will show the printer to be installed.*

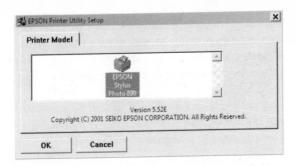

7 *Click on* **OK** *to proceed. You will be prompted to connect the printer to the port. Do this and turn it on. The installer will work for a few seconds before confirming that the new printer is installed and working.*

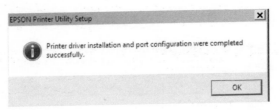

8 *Click on* **OK** *and the job is done.*

As an additional step you can navigate to the Devices and Printers page in the Control Panel to check that your new printer is installed as the default printer before you need to use it. If you choose the Printer Properties from the right-click menu you can also print a test page.

Sharing a printer on a network

Sharing a printer on your home network is simple:

1 *Click the* **Devices and Printers** *button on the* **Start** *menu and right-click on the icon for the printer that you want to share.*

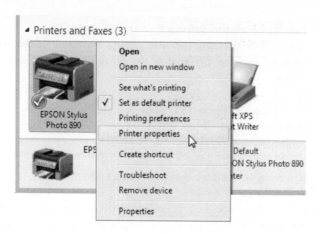

2 *Click on the* **Printer properties** *entry in the middle of the list (not the Properties entry at the bottom) and select the* **Sharing** *tab.*

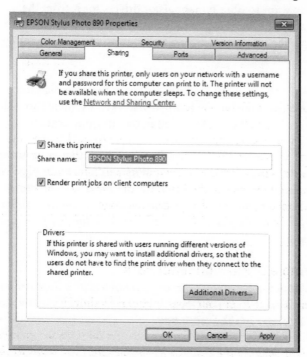

3 *Check the* **Share this printer** *box and click on* **OK** *to confirm. Note that you can also change the name of the share to something different to the default that Windows provides.*

> Note from the last figure that there is a button to install additional drivers for other Windows versions that you may be running on your network.

Installing a network printer is considered in Chapter 17.

Obtaining drivers and manuals

If you have bought your printer from a retailer (local or online) you may want to obtain manuals or drivers for it from the manufacturer's website. You may simply want to be sure that you have the very latest drivers for your printer and operating system.

Obviously, the exact procedures will vary between manufacturers and possibly, models. The following worked example shows how to do this for the Epson 890 used in the previous example.

1 *The first thing to do, of course, is to check the exact name and model number of the printer. With this information, go to the manufacturer's website. In this example it is www.epson.com. You will be prompted for your region and country. Having selected these, you will be transferred to another page within the site.*

Drivers
2 *Within the page you will see a section entitled Support with a Search box to find support for your product. Type the name of the printer in the Search box.*

Find support for any product

3 *Click on the link to your printer. This will take you to the appropriate page:*

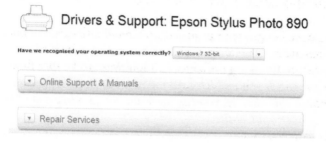

4 *Check that you have the correct version of the operating system, then click on the Online Support and Manuals section.*

5 *Click on the Drivers and Software option.*

6 *Click on the* **Download** *button. This will start a download of a binary driver file that you can click in order to start the installation of the drivers.*

Manuals

7 *Further down the Drivers and Support page there is an entry for Online Support and Manuals. Click on this, then scroll down to the section shown in the following figure:*

Online Manual   **Downloadable Manuals**

8 *Here you can look at an online manual or download three manuals. One of these is a compressed (.zip format) archive which Windows can unpack. The others are in .pdf format, for which you will need Adobe Acrobat Reader. If you do not have this already, you can need download a free copy from the adobe.com website.*

What to do if your printer doesn't work

Most printing problems are printer problems. As with most things, the first thing to do is to check the obvious: is the printer turned on and connected to the PC? Does it have paper in the feed tray? Are there any lights flashing that might indicate that one or more of the ink cartridges are empty? If you have more than one printer on the system make sure you are printing to the correct one!

If you have sent a print job to the printer, you should see a printer icon in the Notification Area at the bottom right end of the Taskbar (this is sometimes referred to by the older name of the System Tray). Clicking on this icon will bring up the Print Queue for your printer as shown in the following figure.

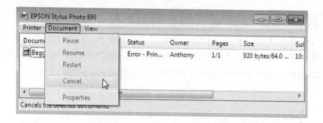

From here you can obtain information about the print job, pause it, restart it, or cancel it altogether. Sometimes, cancelling the print job altogether, then starting afresh by printing from the application will be sufficient to fix the problem.

Having checked the obvious again you can uninstall and reinstall the printer drivers. If this doesn't work, you probably have hardware problems that are beyond the scope of what a home user can do. If your printer is something big, or expensive, or is still under warranty it may be worth calling in outside Help. On the other hand, this may be a good time to buy something new!

THINGS TO REMEMBER

1 Windows 7 will Plug and Play most popular printers – attach your printer to the port, power up and see what happens before trying anything else.

2 Inkjet printers usually have built-in (firmware) routines to clean the print heads. They usually have additional cleaning routines that are bundled with the drivers.

3 Poor quality prints from laser printers are commonly caused by using the wrong type of paper. Try opening a new pack of standard photocopy paper before trying anything else.

4 Most printing problems are printer problems. Check the obvious first:
   ▶ Is the power on?
   ▶ Is there a working connection to the PC?
   ▶ Is there paper in the tray?
   ▶ Is there ink/toner in the cartridges?

12

Components and programs

In this chapter you will learn:
- *how to add, change or remove programs*
- *how to add or remove Windows features*
- *about program access and defaults*

ADDING AND REMOVING APPLICATIONS

To get the best out of your system you need to be able to modify applications such as Windows Live Mail, or third-party applications such as your word processing package. It is also useful to be able to determine which program is used for what purpose when you click on its icon and to control which Windows services are available.

Fortunately, all of these capabilities are available through the Programs section of the Control Panel.

If you are making anything but the most trivial changes it is a sensible precaution to create a System restore point. See Chapter 2 if you need to refresh your memory on how to do this.

REMOVING PROGRAMS

1 *Navigate to* **Control Panel > Programs** *and click on the link* **Uninstall a Program.** *This will list the applications installed on your system:*

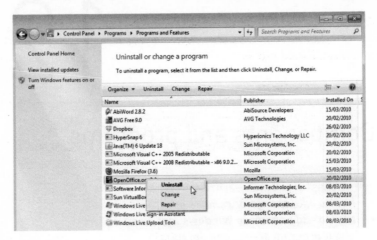

In this instance there are options to Uninstall, Change or Repair; many programs have only the Uninstall option.

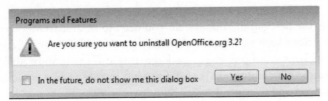

2 *Click on the Uninstall option and click on* **Yes** *if you wish to proceed. This will give control to the installer program for the application and you will probably receive a warning message from Windows like this:*

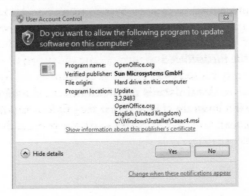

3 *Click on* **Yes** *in order to proceed. Windows will now work for a minute or two before confirming the completion of the uninstallation process.*

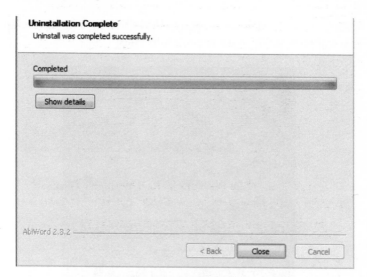

4 *Click on the* **Close** *button and the job is done.*

Note: you may be prompted to reboot your system to complete the Uninstall process.

Most uninstallers will work more or less as described in this example, though not all are particularly well written. The step of shutting down running processes may not be built in and you may receive an error message along the lines of 'This program is currently in use by another process'. If this happens you may have to exit the uninstaller and turn off the offending process. This is frequently caused by Quick Launch icons in the System Tray/Notification Area. Usually these can be turned off by right-clicking on the icon in the tray and selecting **Exit** or **Quit**. If this doesn't work then you may have to kill off the process through the Windows Task Manager.

WINDOWS TASK MANAGER

There are three ways of accessing the Task Manager.

Method 1 is to hold down the **[Ctrl]+[Alt]+[Del]** keys simultaneously. This will present with a list of choices like this:

Click on **Start Task Manager**.

Method 2 is to access the Task Manager through the Control Panel. Although the Task Manager is not explicitly listed in the Control Panel interface, searching on 'task manager' will take you to a link View Running Processes with Task Manager.

Method 3 is to right-click on the Taskbar and select Task Manager from the menu.

Whichever route you choose you will see a list of running programs
and processes and you will have the opportunity to kill them off.

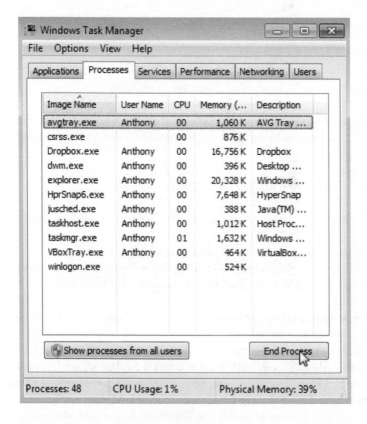

To do this, highlight the relevant entry in the list and click **End
Process**. If you do this, you receive a warning that ending a process
may destabilize the system. This may be the case, especially if you

have chosen the wrong process! However, any damage done will only affect the current session and can be reversed by rebooting your PC.

Finally, no matter how well written the uninstaller there may be some redundant files, probably in a folder in C:/Program Files. These can be manually deleted or left in place as you choose. Leaving them in place will use a small amount of disk space but will not otherwise affect your system.

Installing programs

There are three methods of installing a program.

1 Insert an installation CD/DVD in the drive and either wait for it to autorun or navigate to the installer – usually this is called setup.exe.

2 Install from a link on the Internet.

3 Download an installer from the Internet and install from your PC.

Methods 2 and 3 are really quite similar. If you install from a link, Windows downloads the installer program to a temporary location, runs the installer, then cleans up. The advantage of method 3 is that you keep the installer in case it is needed again. If you don't want it on your system you can burn it to CD before removing the original.

INSTALLING ABIWORD – A WORKED EXAMPLE

Abiword is a small lightweight free word-processing application. There are versions available for Windows, Linux and Mac systems. To obtain a copy go to:

www.abisource.com/download

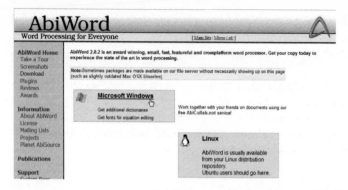

Click on the link to download the Windows version and choose the **Save File** option. By default this will download to your Download folder, but you can change this if you wish.

There's another Office

Abiword is a lightweight free word-processor. If you want a full featured cross-platform Office Suite (free) as a drop-in replacement for the Microsoft Office suite a good choice is Open Office from www.openoffice.org.

To install Abiword on your system:

1 *Click on the installer icon to start the installation process. You will see the standard Windows warning about an 'unknown publisher'. Click on* **Yes** *to proceed.*
2 *Select a language for the installer then click on* **OK** *to continue. This will start the Installation Wizard.*

3 *Click on the* **Next** *button for the next five screens and allow the installer to run to completion.*

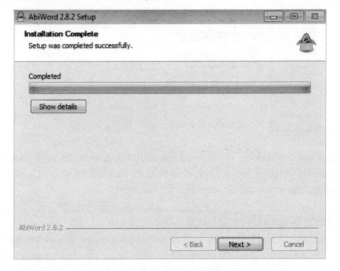

4 *Click the* **Next** *button, then the* **Finish** *button to complete the process and start the newly installed program.*

POST-INSTALLATION JOBS

If you haven't already done so, start Abiword and select **Tools > Preferences** from the menu. You will see something like this:

As you can see, you can set preferences for measurement units, screen colour, interface language, etc. – most of the features that you would expect from a word processor package. There's also a button to restore default values if you change your mind or make a mess of it.

If you check the Save/Save As options from the File menu you will see that Abiword saves files in its own format by default but offers other choices such as .doc (Word compatible) or .pdf. There is, however, no way of changing the default file format from within the Abiword program. Doubtless this oversight will be fixed in a later version (this is free software under development).

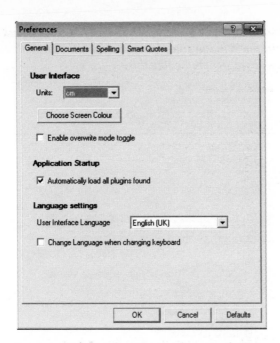

Meanwhile – for those who are interested – here's a hack to fix it. Note: Abiword must not be running while you do this.

1 *Search on 'profile' in the* **Start** *menu Search box.*
2 *Click on the file Abiword.Profile from the list. Windows will report that it is unable to open the file.*

3 *Choose the* **Select a program from a list** *option and click on* OK.

4 *Accept the Windows suggestion to open the file with Notepad. You will see something like this:*

```
AbiWord.Profile - Notepad
File  Edit  Format  View  Help
<!-- ======================================================================= -->
<!-- This file contains AbiSuite Preferences.  AbiSuite is a suite of Open   -->
<!-- Source desktop applications developed by AbiSource, Inc.  Information   -->
<!-- about this application can be found at http://www.abisource.com         -->
<!-- You should not edit this file by hand.                                  -->
<!-- ======================================================================= -->

<!--        Build_ID       = unknown -->
<!--        Build_Version  = 2.8.2 -->
<!--        Build_CompileTime = 12:15:54 -->
<!--        Build_CompileDate = Feb 12 2010 -->

<AbiPreferences app="AbiWord" ver="1.0">

        <Select
                scheme="_custom_"
                autosaveprefs="1"
                useenvlocale="1"
        />

        <!-- The following scheme, _builtin_, contains the built-in application
        **** defaults and adjusted by the installation system defaults.  This scheme
        **** is only written here as a reference.  Any schemes following this one
        **** only list values that deviate from the built-in values.
        **** Items values must observe XML encoding for double quote (&quot;),
        **** ampersand (&amp;), and angle brackets (&lt; and &gt;).
        -->

        <Scheme
                name="_builtin_"
                ColorRevision4="9eb345"
                ToolbarLayouts="FileEditOps FormatOps TableOps ExtraOps"
                ZoomPercentage="100"
                ColorHdrFtr="000000"
                ChangeLangWithKeyboard="0"
                AutoGrammarCheck="0"
                ColorMargin="7f7f7f"
                RulerUnits="cm"
                ColorRevision5="0fb305"
                ZoomType="width"
                ColorImage="0000ff"
                UseGlyphShapingForHebrew="0"
                CustomSmartQuotes="0"
                />
```

5 *Ignore the warning not to edit the file manually and enter this line near the bottom of the* <Scheme> *tag like this:*

```
<Scheme
        name="_custom_"
        ZoomPercentage="148"
        DefaultSaveFormat=".doc"
        />
```

6 *Save the changed file.*

7 *Start Abiword and select* **Save** *from the* **File** *menu.*

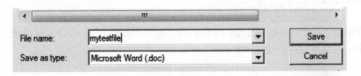

File name:	mytestfile	Save
Save as type:	Microsoft Word (.doc)	Cancel

As you can see the new default file format for saving is .doc.

Turn Windows features on or off

Most of the Windows features are set to default values that suit most users and are probably best left alone. The two entries that are most likely to be of interest are Games and Internet Explorer. The link to turn Windows features on or off is in Control Panel > Programs and Features.

As you can see, features are turned on/off by ticking/unticking boxes and saving your changes.

Default programs

There are three headings in the Control Panel > Programs > Default Programs section. They are:

▶ *Change default settings for media or devices.*
▶ *Make a file type always open in a specific program.*
▶ *Set your default programs.*

This is simply a short-cut to the Autoplay section in the Control Panel > Hardware and Sound section which we considered in Chapter 3.

MAKE A FILE TYPE ALWAYS OPEN IN A SPECIFIC PROGRAM

Windows 'knows' which application program to use to open a file by checking the file extension. A file name consists of some letters that mean something to the human reader followed by a (usually three-letter) extension. A file called Chapter-12.doc, for example will (in all probability) contain the text of Chapter 12 and its extension – the .doc bit – tells Windows that this is a word-processor file which is compatible with Microsoft Word. On most Window systems the file extension is hidden from you the user, but is visible behind the scenes to Windows.

If you want to make file extensions visible on your system open the Control Panel and search on 'file extension'. This will take you to **Folder Options**. Click on the link **Show or Hide File Extensions** and uncheck the box marked **Hide Extensions for Known File Types**.

Changing the default file type / application association

Most of the time, file extensions work quietly behind the scenes to make sure that the 'right' application opens the chosen file type. For example, .doc files may be associated with Microsoft Word or, as in this example, with the Writer component of Open Office. However, you may want to change this. For example, if you have downloaded and installed Abiword you may want to use this as the new default program for opening .doc files. Here's how:

1 *Navigate to* **Control Panel > Programs > Default Programs** *and click on the link to* **Make a file type always open in a specific program**. *You will see a list of file extensions and associations.*

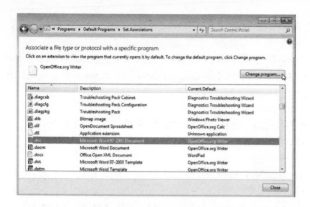

2 Scroll down the alphabetic list until you find the .doc file extension, then click on the **Change program** button. This will show the present association and some recommendations. Unfortunately Abiword is not listed here so we will have to search for it.

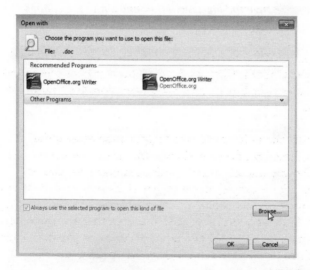

3 Click on the **Browse** button and you will be taken to the Program Files section of the file system. From here, navigate to the file AbiWord.exe. Highlight it and click on the **Open** button. (Note that for this exercise the show file extensions option is ON)

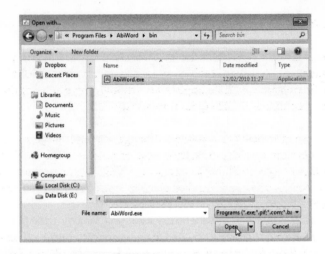

4   This will take you to a list of other programs. Highlight
    Abiword in the list and click on the **OK** button. Windows will
    now change the file association and show the change in the
    default list.

5   To check that the change has really worked, click on any
    .doc file and it should open with Abiword.

SET YOUR DEFAULT PROGRAMS

This is really a variant on the file associations that we have just considered. However, it allows you to associate a group of file types/extensions with an application (though there is an option to deal with individual file types if necessary).

A common reason for wanting to change a default program is replacing Internet Explorer with another browser such as Firefox or Opera (both available as free downloads). If, for example you have downloaded and installed Firefox, you may want to use it in place of Internet Explorer. Here's how:

1 *Navigate to* **Control Panel > Programs > Default Programs** *and click on the link to* **Set your default programs**. *You will see a list like the one in the following figure:* 12.21

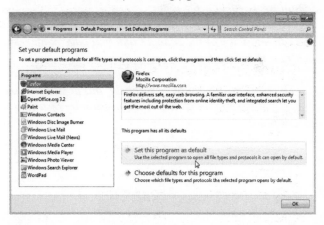

2 *Select the program that you want to use as the new default – in this case Firefox – and click on* **Set this program as default**. *Then click on* **OK** *to finish. Firefox is now your default browser.*

THINGS TO REMEMBER

1 *Before making any but minor changes to your system it is sensible to set a system restore point.*

2 *If you can't find what you want in the Control Panel you can use the Search option to look up keywords such as 'file associations'.*

3 *When uninstalling a program you may need to use Task Manager to kill off running processes first.*

4 *After you have uninstalled a program you may have to reboot the system and/or manually remove leftover files.*

5 *After installing a program you may need to set it as the new default for particular file types.*

6 *You can undo any of the changes that you have made – so don't be afraid to have a go.*

7 *If it all goes horribly wrong – unlikely, but possible – you can always roll back to an earlier configuration by restoring to a restore point.*

13

Installing/reinstalling Windows

In this chapter you will learn:
- *how to avoid a reinstall*
- *how to prepare for a reinstall*
- *how to perform an OEM and a conventional install*
- *what to do after the installation*

How to avoid a reinstall

Installing or reinstalling the Windows operating system is not an everyday task. However, it is something that you may have to do after a very severe virus infection, for example, or a hard disk failure.

Installing or reinstalling Windows is neither difficult nor complicated. However, it is time-consuming and will destroy all the contents of your hard disk so before doing anything make sure that you have an up-to-date backup of all your data. You should also try restoring a couple of test files from your backup just to make sure that the backup system is working 100%. Even key settings like your e-mail server addresses, dialup numbers and so forth can be replaced by various means, but data, once gone, is gone for good.

If your system has become corrupt because of some recent change, you can, of course, roll it back to a previous known good state by using the System Restore utility which we considered in Chapter 2.

Another quick and easy fix for a damaged system is the System File Check utility. To use this utility you will need to launch a command prompt with Administrator privileges. To do this type 'CMD' in the Search box on the **Start** menu. This will show the CMD program at the top of the list. Right-click on this and choose the Run as Administrator option.

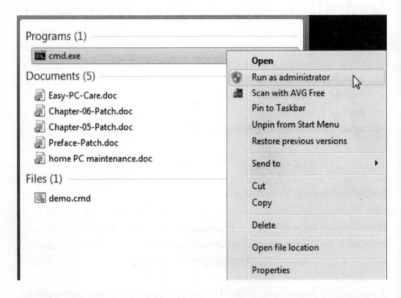

You will be asked to confirm that you want to run the program with these privileges. Click on the **Yes** button to do this. The SFC utility will start and report its progress in percentage terms.

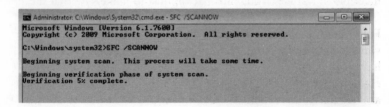

The System File Check process will probably take several minutes to run; Windows is checking all protected system files and will attempt to automatically replace any that have become corrupt. You may be prompted to provide the original installation disk at some point in the process.

After running the System File Check, reboot the PC – it's always good practice to reboot after making any changes – and test for stability and proper operation. If your system is now working properly then you won't need to reinstall Windows. If you are still having problems, you may decide to reinstall. The key to doing this with the minimum of inconvenience to yourself or any other users of the PC is to prepare for the job beforehand.

How to prepare for a reinstall

The key to a successful reinstall is preparation. The first thing to do is a backup of all your data. Providing you have some sort of backup regime in place, this is easy – just run your backup system and put the backup media somewhere safe. (Remember to test!) If you don't have a backup system in place, now might be a good time to set one up – see Chapter 6. Alternatively, you may like to use Windows Easy Transfer – more on this later.

As a further preparation, check that you have any software drivers for peripheral devices such as printers, scanners, external modems and so forth. If anything is missing or out of date, now is the time to visit manufacturers' websites in order to download what is needed and burn it to CD or other removable storage.

Finally, make sure that you have a record of any setting that you want to save and restore. As a minimum you should be sure to have user names, passwords, access codes, etc. so that you can connect to the Internet and send and receive e-mail. That way, you are not too far from help if you need it. You could use Windows Easy Transfer for this but this is putting rather a lot of eggs in the same electronic basket. There are some key settings that are best kept as ink on paper in a safe place.

DATA

This is straightforward. Use your existing backup system to make sure that you have a fully up-to-date backup of your data. If you don't have a system for doing this, save the essential files to a removable medium such as CD/DVD, a pen drive, an external hard disk or another machine on your network if you have one. Alternatively, you could use the Easy Transfer Wizard.

DRIVERS

Check that you have driver or installation disks for printers, modem, etc. and download anything you need (or may need) from manufacturers' websites.

SETTINGS

You should write down the settings that you need to access the Internet and to send and receive e-mail. Your user name and password for Internet access will probably be with the documentation that you received when the connection was first set up. If you can't find what you need, a phone call or an e-mail to the support staff at your Internet Service Provider (ISP) should do the trick. If you have lost your password, they will not be able to recover it for you, but providing that you can prove who you are, they can probably reset it for you.

Your key e-mail settings are: your user name, password and server addresses. You may be able to obtain these from your e-mail provider (as often as not this will be your ISP) either by a call or an e-mail to their Help Desk or by visiting their website and looking for a 'settings' page. In addition to your user name and password for e-mail, you will also need the addresses of two mail servers which are used for sending and receiving e-mail. For most users these are in the form of:

pop3.yourisp.com (for incoming mail)

and

smtp.yourisp.com (for outgoing mail)

Depending on your provider, these servers may have slightly different names like mail.yourisp.com or relay.yourisp.com – check with your service provider or dig around in your e-mail program to find the information that you need.

To find your e-mail settings in Windows Live Mail:

1 *Start the program by clicking on its icon.*
2 *Right-click on the e-mail account that you want to examine and select* **Properties** *from the context menu.*

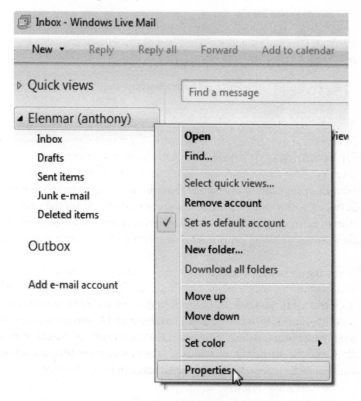

3 *Select the* **Servers** *tab:*
4 *Make a note of the information that you need.*

Elenmar (anthony) Properties

| General | Servers | Connection | Security | Advanced |

Server Information

My incoming mail server is a [POP3] server.

Incoming mail (POP3): pop3.elenmar.com

Outgoing mail (SMTP): smtp.elenmar.com

Incoming Mail Server

E-mail username: elenmar

Password: •••••••

☑ Remember password

Windows Easy Transfer

This utility is really intended for moving files and settings from an old PC to a new one but it can also be used to back up data and settings before a reinstall. Note that for purposes of backup the PC that you are working on is the OLD machine.

To use the Transfer Wizard:

1 *Type 'easy transfer' in the Search box on the* **Start** *menu, then click on the Windows Easy Transfer program in the listing at the top of the menu. This will take you to the Welcome screen.*
2 *Read the introductory material, then click on the* **Next** *button. You will be presented with three options:*
   ▷ *An Easy Transfer cable*
   ▷ *Network*
   ▷ *External disk or USB drive.*
3 *Both the Cable and Network options are unsuitable for our present purposes so we will use the disk/USB option. The*

process is much the same as any other backup: copying data and settings to an independent destination which will later become the source from which the data and settings will be restored. Click on the External Hard Disk or USB Flash Drive option.

4 *At the next screen you will be asked to specify whether this is the New or the Old computer. Select the second option – Old – and click on it. Windows will examine the system and list everything available for backup.*

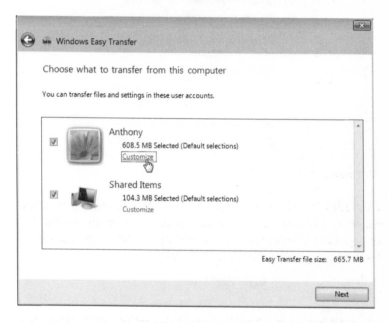

5 *Note from the figure that there is an option to customize the selection. If you select this option you will see something like this:*

6 *If you already have adequate backups of data files such as your documents, music, pictures, etc., you may want to uncheck these and only back up the settings. This will, of course, save storage space and time. Note, too, from the figure that there is an Advanced option which will give you even greater control over your selections. When you have made your choices click on **Next**.*

7 At the next screen you have the opportunity to set a password for your backup. Do this – or not as you choose – then click on the **Save** button. This will take you to a screen where you choose the target drive for your backup.

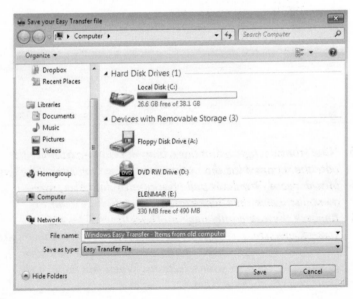

8 *As you can see from the figure we have a choice of:*
  ▷ *Floppy drive A:*
  ▷ *DVD drive D:*
  ▷ *USB flash drive E:*
In practice, the floppy drive is unlikely to have sufficient storage capacity to be useful so the choice is either DVD or USB drive. If you choose DVD, then Windows will open the drive tray and prompt you for a disk.
9 *Having decided on your target drive, highlight it and click on the* **Open** *button. Windows will start the backup process and output a progress report as it does so.*

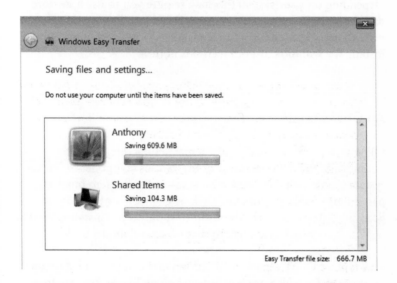

10 *When the process is complete, click on the* **Next** *button and note the reported location of your backup, then click the* **Next** *button again. Windows will now confirm that the process is complete. Click the* **Close** *button.*
11 *Remove the disk containing your backup and store it somewhere safe.*

Whatever method or combination of methods you used, you should now have a backup of key information from your PC:

- ▶ *data*
- ▶ *drivers*
- ▶ *settings.*

With this information gathered and safely stored you are ready to begin the relatively straightforward process of installing Windows. Depending on your system this may require you to use a Restore disk from the PC manufacturer – an OEM install – or you may need to use a branded Microsoft installation disk – a conventional install. We will look at both methods in turn.

An OEM install

OEM stands for Original Equipment Manufacturer. This term does not indicate the manufacturers of the various components, but the system builder who assembled them into a PC. System builders – particularly the large ones like Dell, or Compaq – often have a licensing agreement with Microsoft to supply a pre-installed version of Windows which is specific to that make and model of PC.

This type of OEM version of Windows is usually provided on one (or more) CDs which are labelled something like System Restore disks. They contain an image of the installed system and are flashed onto the hard drive in order to restore your PC to the state that it was in when it left the factory. When you run a Restore of this type, you will restore the operating system along with any other pre-installed software that may have been bundled with the system when you bought it. This is a rather inflexible approach, but it has the advantage of being very easy to do.

The first thing to do is to read the instructions! Although there are generic similarities between Restore Disks there may be differences of detail between different manufacturers. Generally speaking, however, unless the instructions from the manufacturer state otherwise, put the Restore Disk in the CD-ROM drive on your PC, restart the PC and follow the instructions on screen.

Depending on the speed of your system, the largely automated process of restoring the system may take anything up to an hour. When you are finished, remove the Restore Disk and put it somewhere safe – you may need it again one day. Having done this, you will need to restore your backed-up data and settings. See the Post Install section below.

A conventional install

CHECKING CMOS/BIOS SETTINGS

Before you start an install there are a couple of things worth checking in the CMOS setup utility. The section on how to access the BIOS/CMOS settings in Chapter 6 describes how to do this.

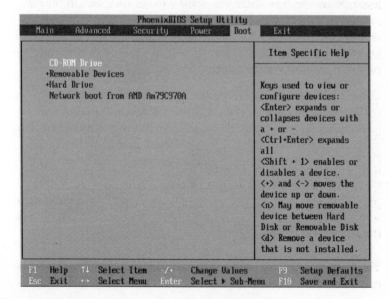

Once you are in the setup utility, you are interested in two items: the boot order of the PC and the status of CMOS anti-virus checking. Both of these settings can be important for the install process.

If there is an anti-virus function in the CMOS setup and it is set to Enabled, then change it to Disabled. The reason is that the Windows Installer will write to system areas of your hard disk as part of the installation process and this could look like virus activity to the anti-virus utility.

The boot order is the order in which the system looks at the various drives as it starts up. To boot to, and install from, a CD or DVD, the boot order in CMOS needs to be set so that the system looks at the CD or DVD drive first. The figure above shows how this is done in a setup screen for a Phoenix BIOS.

To navigate within the setup utility you will need to use the arrow keys to move the cursor (there's no mouse support in most CMOS setup utilities) and other keys as instructed in the Help screens. Here, we use the left and right arrow keys to move along the menu at the top and the up and down ones to move up and down the menus. In the example, the CDROM drive is first in the list on the **Boot** menu which is where you want it to be. Any item in the list may be promoted with [+] or demoted with [–]. When you have set the boot order to what you want – in this case CD-ROM, Hard Drive, Removable Drive as shown is ideal – exit from the setup program and save your changes.

Other BIOS manufacturers use their own interfaces to the setup utility, so if you have (say) an AMI or AWARD BIOS they will have the facility to change the boot order but they may use entirely different ways of achieving it. Experiment – and don't forget the Quit without saving option if you get yourself into a mess!

Installing Windows 7

Windows 7 has the most straightforward installer of any Windows version to date. In outline, all you do is put the DVD in the drive, boot the PC and follow the instructions on the screen. There are some extra steps if you are installing to a disk that has already had a copy of Windows on it.

If you are re-installing to a hard disk that has a previous installation of Windows on it you can avoid the Extra Steps For a Used Disk by using a third party software such as Partition Magic to remove existing disk partitions before starting the installer.

1 *Put the Windows installation DVD in the drive and reboot the PC. If you are prompted to Press any Key to boot to CD or DVD this means that there is an existing installation on the hard disk. Press any key as requested otherwise the system will start to boot to the old Windows installation. If you are installing to an empty hard disk this message won't appear. Either way, as the PC starts up it will run the installer from the DVD drive. This process may take a minute or two.*

2 *At the next screen, select the language settings for where you live from the drop-down list. Then click on the* Next *button to continue.*
3 *At the next screen, click on* Install now.
4 *This will take you to the Licence Agreement. Tick the box to agree to the terms of the End User Licence Agreement (EULA) and click on the* Next *button to continue.*
5 *At the next screen you will be asked to confirm the type of installation that you want to carry out. Choose the Custom (Advanced) option by clicking on it to proceed.*

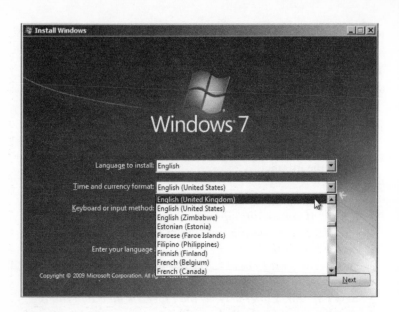

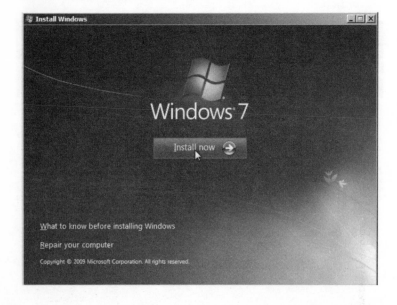

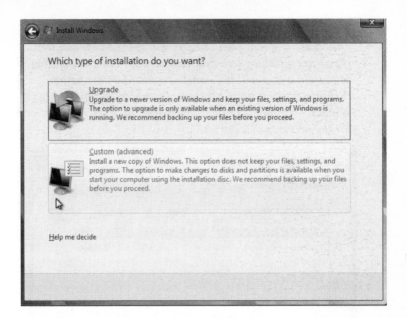

6 *If you are installing to a new or empty disk you will see a screen like this:*

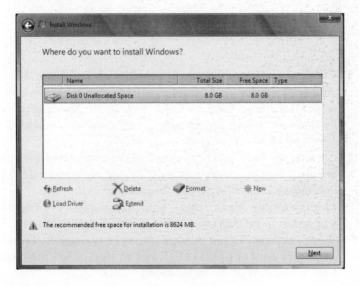

If this is your situation then you can jump forward to step 9. Otherwise you will need to carry out these additional steps.

7 *If you are installing to a disk that already has an operating system on it you will see something like the next figure. It shows the partitions left from a previous installation of Windows 7. These need to be removed in order to make room for the new installation.*

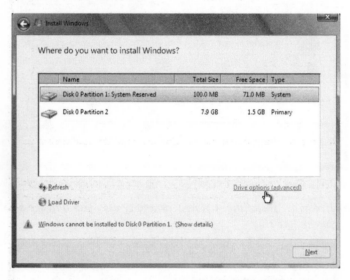

8 *Click on the Drive Options (Advanced) link and delete the old partitions. For each partition you want to delete you will receive a warning. Click on* **OK** *to remove the highlighted partition and repeat for any other partition(s) until you see a screen like the one in step 6.*

9 *Click on the* **Next** *button to install to the unallocated space on the disk. Windows will now begin the 'big copy' phase of the installation and will report its progress like this:*

10 *This is a lengthy process and – note from the figure – Windows will restart more than once in the course of the installation. When this happens you may see (briefly) a message to 'Press any key to boot to CD/DVD'. Don't do this – it will take you back to the start of the installation process.*

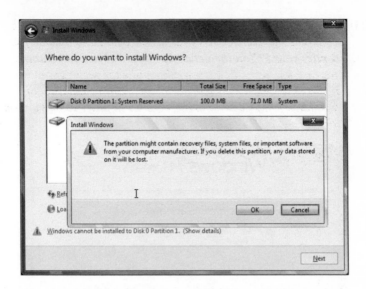

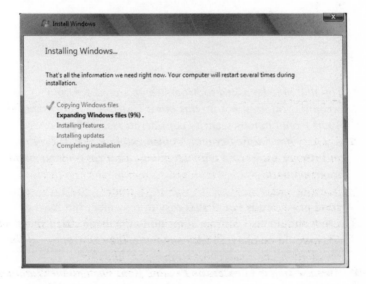

As the installation proceeds you will see various progress messages which require no action from you, so feel free to take a break until the next stage.

11 *With the system largely in place it is time to set up a user account. Enter a name for your user account and a name to identify your PC on the network. Click on* **Next** *to proceed.*

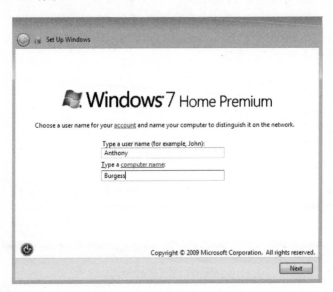

12 *You will now be asked to provide a password for your account. You need not do this but it is strongly recommended. Apart from obvious security considerations, without one, you may have difficulty with implementing Parental Controls on Internet access and with accessing resources on your own home network.*

A good password is one that is easy to remember but hard to guess. It should also contain some non-alphabetic characters. Friday would be okay, Friday;-999 would be better.

13 *The next step is to enter the Product Key. The Product Key should be on the packaging of the installation disk. Enter it carefully. Note the option (tick box) to* **Automatically activate Windows when I'm online.** *If you choose not to do this at installation time you can do so later through the Control Panel within a month of installation.*

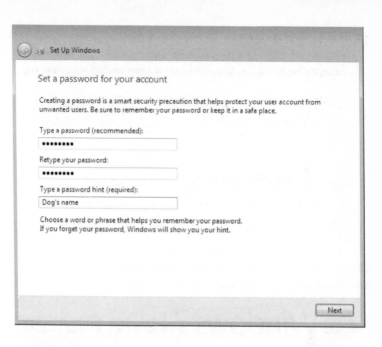

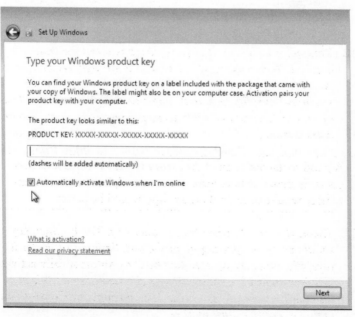

14 *At the next screen you will be asked to choose your automatic update settings. Unless you have reasons not too you should accept the default setting to* **Use recommended settings.**

Help protect your computer and improve Windows automatically

Use recommended settings
Install important and recommended updates, help make Internet browsing safer, check online for solutions to problems, and help Microsoft improve Windows.

Install important updates only
Only install security updates and other important updates for Windows.

Ask me later
Until you decide, your computer might be vulnerable to security threats.

15 *Confirm date, time and time zone settings.*

16 *Windows will now finalize your settings:*

Windows 7 Home Premium

Windows is finalizing your settings

17 *After this there will be a couple more screens – Welcome and Preparing Your Desktop – which require no input from you. Remove the installation disk from the DVD drive and store it somewhere safe. Reboot the system, log in and start the Post-install tasks.*

Post-install

RESTORING WITH THE EASY TRANSFER WIZARD

If you used the Easy Transfer wizard to back up your settings and/ or data, now is the time to restore them.

1 *Start the Easy Transfer wizard (search on 'easy transfer' in the Control Panel if necessary).*
2 *Click on* **Next** *at the Welcome screen.*
3 *Choose the external hard disk USB option.*
4 *Click on the (default) New computer option, then select* **Yes** *at the next screen. You will see the attached disk drives including the one that has your transfer data.*

neither of the options in steps 3 or 4 appear on screen so I don't know whether/which bit to capitalize
5 *Click on the drive which has the data (in this case E:) to view its contents and verify that this is the correct drive.*

Name	Date modified
Windows Easy Transfer - Items from old ...	19/03/2010 10:54

6 *Highlight the backup file, then click on the* **Open** *button at the bottom of the window. This will show the files available for restoring. Note there is an* **Advanced** *option which allows you to fine tune your choices. When you have made your selection, click on the* **Transfer** *button to continue. Windows will now transfer your files and settings. You will be warned not to use your computer until the transfer is complete.*

> ☑   Anthony
>   400.3 MB Selected (Default selections)
>   Customize
>
> Easy Transfer file size: 400.3 MB
> Advanced Options

7 *When the transfer is complete you will be given the opportunity to check what files have been restored. When you have finished with this, click the* **Close** *button and the job is done.*

WHAT TO DO IF THE WIZARD HASN'T WORKED

1 *If, for any reason, the Wizard fails (and they sometimes do!) or you chose to back up your files and settings manually, you will need to restore them manually. The exact order in which you do this isn't particularly important. You may restore your files from the backup medium and then do the settings or you may chose to reinstate your settings first.*

2 To restore your files, run the Restore option of whatever backup method you used to save them. This may be simply copying from removable media such as a CD or a pen drive, or you may have used the backup facilities provided with Windows. Whatever your backup system, now is the time to put its Restore facilities to the test. You may want to refer back to Chapter 6, to remind yourself of the details.

3 With your data files restored, you need to restore your other settings – particularly the settings needed to connect to the Internet and e-mail servers.

4 To connect to the Internet you will probably need to reinstall your modem. If you have a setup disk from the supplier, use it. If you need to do this by hand, skip forward to Chapter 15, and follow the instructions for your modem type. You will need your user name and password for this – that's why you wrote them down – old fashioned ink on paper instead of trusting a Wizard!

5 With your Internet connection in place and working, you will need to set up your e-mail program. Again, if you wrote down the settings on paper, this is easy enough to do. The figures on pages 183 and 184 walked you through the process of collecting this information from Windows Live Mail – all you now need to do is to restore them. If you are using a different e-mail program, such as the increasingly popular (and free) Thunderbird you will have to dig around in the interface to restore your settings.

6 With Internet connectivity and e-mail restored, this may be a good time to run the Windows Update service – there have probably been a lot of critical updates since you bought your PC and they will have been lost in the process of reinstalling. Note that if you chose the default setting to Use Recommended Settings at step 13 of the installation process above Windows will automatically update itself when you connect to the Internet. If, for any reason this doesn't happen, you can view or change your settings in **Control Panel > System and Security > Windows Update** or click on the **Check for Updates** option to launch the process manually.

REINSTALLING YOUR APPLICATIONS

The final essential task is to reinstall your applications programs and tweaking Windows – refer back to Chapter 12, if you have any doubts about how to go about this.

Two final optional tasks may be to defragment your hard disk and manually set a system restore point. Installer programs use a lot of temporary files as they work and delete them when they finish, often leaving a badly fragmented disk and even leftover temporary files. Setting a system restore point, can also save a lot of driver reinstalling, etc. should you need to make changes in the next day or so.

This may be a good time to go back to Chapter 1.

THINGS TO REMEMBER

1 *Reinstalling Windows removes everything from your hard drive so preparation is essential before you start.*

2 *Backup your files and test your backup before committing yourself.*

3 *Keep a separate record – preferably ink on paper – of key settings such as e-mail and Internet access.*

4 *Try running a System File Check (SFC) before reinstalling. You may be able to avoid a reinstall altogether.*

5 *Check that you have your Windows Product Key to hand before starting an install.*

6 *Both Windows Backup and the Easy Transfer wizard will store your data in proprietary file formats. Simple copies of files on removable drives are easily accessible on another system (even a non-Windows system) if things go wrong.*

14

....

Troubleshooting

In this chapter you will learn:
- *about the troubleshooting wizards*
- *how to gather the facts and use the diagnostic tools*
- *how to make a list of possibilities and test them out*
- *Some common problems and their solutions*

Sooner or later you will be faced with a machine that just won't work. You will have tried everything that you can think of, looked at the manuals and e-mailed your friends, but still, it just won't work. What's needed now, is not an encyclopaedia of PC problems (which would have to be a very big book to list all of them!) but a systematic approach to fault diagnosis.

The Troubleshooting wizards

The System and Security section of the Control Panel has a link: Find and Fix Problems. If you click on this link you will be presented with an array of possible problem areas.

Each of the links in the figure points to a wizard application which takes you through a series of screens gathering information, requiring you to select various options, then running a diagnostic test:

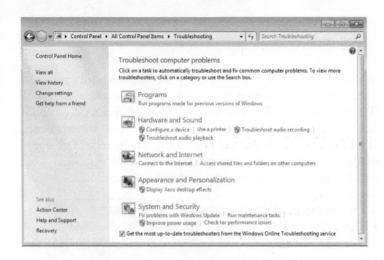

Detecting issues

before producing a report or suggesting a fix for the problem.

Install a driver for this device

The driver for Multimedia Audio Controller is not installed. Install the latest driver for the device.

➔ Apply this fix

➔ Skip this fix
Continue troubleshooting without applying this fix.

This is great when it works. But if it doesn't, you need to adopt a rather more systematic hands-on approach.

Using Device Manager

Device Manager gives an overview of all installed hardware and highlights and problems that it detects. It also provides some tools that you can use to fix any reported problems. It can't detect and fix everything, but it is a good starting point if you are experiencing problems. You can find a link to it in **Control Panel > Hardware and Sound > Devices and Printers,** or you can use the Search box with the search term 'device manger' to find it.

Where there are no problems the list of devices will be closed up – like the one in the figure above. However, if there are problems the list will be opened up and the problem device will be highlighted like this:

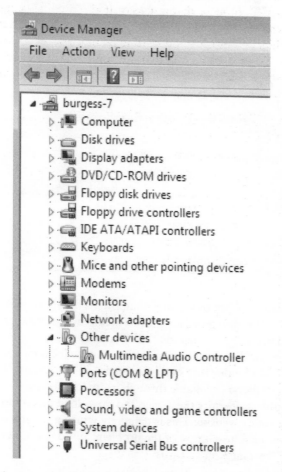

In this instance Windows is reporting problems with a Multimedia Audio Controller. The main symptom that you would observe in this case would be a lack of audio output. The first step to fixing this problem is to right-click on the icon for the suspect device and select properties from the context menu.

As you can see from this figure, Windows is reporting that no
drivers for this device are installed. There is also a button to
Update Driver. If you click on this Windows will give you a choice
to 'Search for drivers online' or to 'Browse the local file system' for
drivers. The obvious first step is to try the online update. Windows
has a lot of drivers available through its update service or may
even be able to identify the device and download drivers from the
manufacturer's website. This is definitely worth a try and often
leads to a quick resolution of the problem. If it doesn't work then
you will see a message like this:

Windows was unable to install your Multimedia Audio Controller

Windows could not find driver software for your device.

If you know the manufacturer of your device, you can visit its website and check the support
section for driver software.

The next step for your enquiries is to identify the card manufacturer and visit their website. If all else fails you may need to power down the PC, remove the device and check for a manufacturer's name and any serial numbers that are on the product. Armed with this information, replace the device and reboot the machine, go to the manufacturer's website and download the necessary drivers.

There are third-party sites which provide drivers that have been uploaded by other users. Most of these sites are reputable and derive their income from advertising but, as always, exercise care and virus scan anything that you download before installing it on your system.

Once you have downloaded and checked your drivers – the default location for this is your Download folder – you will probably need to unzip them so that the installer becomes visible to Windows. Once this is done you can install by clicking on the installer program. This is usually called setup.exe

Autorun	22/03/2010 08:23	Icon	98 KB
AUTORUN	13/06/2000 14:59	Setup Information	1 KB
CmiOemConfig	22/03/2010 08:23	Configuration sett...	1 KB
CmiSetupConfig.dll	22/03/2010 08:23	Application extens...	3 KB
CmSetx.dll	22/03/2010 08:23	Application extens...	1 KB
CmUtil.dll	22/03/2010 08:23	Application extens...	44 KB
Setup	22/03/2010 08:23	Application	32 KB

Alternatively, you can step through the options in Device Manager and use the browse option to navigate to the installer. Whichever route you choose Windows will output a warning about unsigned drivers – skip over this – and install the necessary software. Once this is done, refresh the view of Device Manager and success will be indicated by a closed-up list like the one shown in the figure on page 206.

If you can't effect a cure through Device Manager or – uncommon but not unknown – the non-functioning device is reported as working when it is not, you may have to start working directly with the hardware and Operating System components. The key to success in this is a systematic approach.

Isolating the symptom

The modern multimedia PC is a complex machine. It has many items of hardware (usually from different manufacturers) as well as applications software, device driver software, and so on. The key to successful fault diagnosis is the systematic examination of these in order to isolate and fix the problem.

When diagnosing hardware problems, this usually means removing suspect hardware components one at a time until the problem rights itself. Using this method the last component removed is probably the defective part. Alternatively, some technicians will strip a PC down to its components and reassemble it from first principles, testing each stage of the build as they go. This can be quite a challenge for the home user, but it may be worth the effort. Experience has shown that a radical rebuild will sometimes cause a problem to disappear even though you never found out the exact cause – there are so many components, so many possibilities for a bad contact between components that a rebuild is quicker than testing every possible bad connection individually.

In terms of software diagnosis, the process is essentially similar – remove any programs that may be running in the background – disconnect from the Internet and turn off your virus checker and firewall, for example – until only the suspect program is running. If, at this stage, the problem persists, try uninstalling the suspect software package. In XP use Control Panel > Add/Remove Programs (in Vista use Control Panel > Programs > Installed Programs) and remove the suspect application. After you have done this – rebooting the machine if necessary – reinstall your application from the original disk. If this fixes the problem – fine. Just don't forget to restart your firewall and virus scanner before reconnecting to the Internet!

With both software and hardware diagnosis, you are making a list – formally on paper or just in your own mind – then working systematically through it, eliminating possibilities in order to isolate and fix the problem.

Separating software from hardware

It is not always easy to tell if a problem is caused by a hardware or a software fault, so there are a handful of things which most technicians find useful.

▶ **Known good hardware.** *If you have a suitable replacement component that is 'known good' – either new or borrowed from a working machine – swap the suspect part for the known good part and if this fixes the problem, then you know which component to replace. This swap out is not always easy for the home user with only one PC. Even so, if for example, you have two sticks of RAM installed and you suspect a memory problem, you can remove one stick and boot the machine using only the other. If it cures the problem, power down and swap the RAM and reboot. If the problem reappears, then you have successfully isolated it and know which RAM stick to replace. (Don't forget anti-static precautions when doing this!)*
▶ **Uninstall/reinstall** – *as noted earlier, uninstalling and reinstalling suspect software can often fix a problem.*
▶ **Patching and upgrading** – *this is particularly applicable to device drivers for hardware components. It is good practice to download patches or upgrades from manufacturers' websites, anyway, and if it helps to fix a problem then it is definitely worthwhile.*
▶ **Virus check** – *at some point it will be necessary to run a full system scan with an up-to-date virus scanner. If a system is functioning reasonably well, or you have reason to suspect a virus, it may be a good idea to start your investigation by*

running a virus scan. You may also like to run a scanner to detect ad-ware, spyware or other 'malware' at the same time. See also Chapter 16.

▶ **Common sense** – *no set of rules or guidelines can provide an alternative to common sense. Think carefully about the problem and make notes if necessary. Assume nothing and always – yes, always – look for the obvious. There is no point in testing the PC's internal power supply unit if the fuse in the plug on the wall has blown!*

Investigating the problem

If you have tried the general approach outlined above and still can't find the answer to the problem, you will need to investigate further and a little more systematically. Imagine that you are working for someone else – a customer – or that you are making a call to a remote Help Desk and you are preparing to answer their probable questions.

DESCRIBE THE PROBLEM

If you were to make a call to a Help Desk you would need to describe the problem to them in both general and specific terms. Go back and review Chapter 4, and step though the sections on *Defining the Problem* and *Gathering the Information*. This exercise will, if nothing else, help you to organize your thoughts.

This is also the time at which you should consider other users of the PC. If you share the machine with other family members – particularly children – you need to enlist their help in finding the cause of the problem. Tact and diplomacy are at least as important as technical knowledge for this undertaking. If you can approach this as simply a problem to be solved, without implying any kind of blame on anyone, you are more likely to win their co-operation and find a solution quickly.

REPRODUCE THE PROBLEM

A problem which has only happened once isn't really a problem –
it's a one-off inconvenience. The first thing to do, then, is to reboot
the PC and reproduce the problem. Do this in a systematic manner,
noting in particular any error messages that the system gives you.
At this stage, the problem and its solution often become apparent –
a missing Desktop shortcut, for example can generally be fixed
either by letting Windows search for the target file, or you may want
to delete the icon and make a new shortcut to your application.

Whatever, the cause, and whatever the cure, always reboot the
machine and test that your fix has worked.

WHAT HAS CHANGED RECENTLY?

Another fruitful line of enquiry when troubleshooting is to ask
(yourself or others) what, if anything, has changed recently.
The fact is that systems which are working properly tend to
go on working properly (though not always, of course!) and
many failures result from changes to the system which have had
unintended consequences.

Systems that have had hardware or software changes are more
likely to manifest faults than those that have been chugging along
quietly for some time. Hardware changes are usually fairly obvious –
if you added a disk drive or fitted some more RAM yesterday and
the PC is playing up today, it is a relatively simple task to reverse
the changes and see if that cures the problem.

Software changes can be more difficult to detect. You may have
downloaded operating system updates, device drivers or utilities
and these may be conflicting with other installed programs. If
someone else who uses the PC has downloaded something, this too,
may be causing you problems.

If you can't track down the problem, and you suspect that it is
software related you can check in Add/Remove Programs to see

if there are any unfamiliar entries, including operating system updates from Microsoft which may have been downloaded and installed as Automatic Updates.

Another place worth checking is System Restore which will list all recent software updates and give you the opportunity to roll back the system to an earlier date.

Hardware problems are most likely to be visible in Device Manager (see the figure on page 207).

A recent change of hardware or software is the most likely cause of a problem but this may not necessarily be the case. For example, if you do a RAM upgrade on your PC and it boots fine afterwards, but crashes after a few minutes then the cause is almost certainly not the memory upgrade. The crash-after-five-minutes symptom is typical of an overheating CPU chip – possibly the CPU fan became disconnected from the motherboard in the course of the memory upgrade. In this case, something has changed of course, but not necessarily the most readily apparent thing.

_____

Diagnostic utilities

DEVICE MANAGER

As noted earlier in the chapter, Device Manager should probably be the first tool that you use to investigate a fault with your PC. It is, as often as not, your last – once you have fixed the problem – a Device Manager that displays a closed-up list is a good indicator that your efforts have been successful.

SYSTEM INFORMATION

This utility is not part of the Control Panel. The easiest way to find it is to search for 'system information' from the **Start** menu. Click

on the link that appears at the top of the menu and you will see
something like:

System Information gives more detailed information than Device
Manager and can be useful for tracking down problems such as
conflicts between devices. It has an Explorer style interface.
The default view – as in the figure above – is a System Summary.
To expand the list in the left pane, click the + signs; the right pane
displays the details of the item selected in the left.

The **Tools** and **View** menus are of interest for troubleshooting
purposes. The Tools menu contains some utilities which are frankly
rather obscure, though you can run **System Restore** from here. The
View menu includes **History** which will give you an indication of
recent changes to the system.

CHECK DISK (CHKDSK.EXE)

CHKDSK is a disk checking utility that has been present in all
Windows versions since the early days. As the name suggests it is
used to check and fix various problems that may arise with your
hard disk. Using CHKDSK is described in Chapter 1, as one of
the 'four useful tools'. This utility can be run from the Windows
Graphical User Interface (GUI) or it can be started from a
command line. This will need Administrator rights so launch your
command processor by right-clicking on the CMD.EXE icon and
choosing Run As Administrator from the context menu.

WINDOWS MEMORY DIAGNOSTIC

This is a utility from Microsoft which is not distributed with
Windows itself, but which can be downloaded from their site free

of charge. You can also download the instructions on how to use it from there. A search on the terms 'Windows memory diagnostic' should find the relevant page. After you have downloaded this utility – a file called MTINST.EXE – click on it to run it. You will be required to accept the standard Microsoft Licence Agreement. Accepting this will take you to a choice between creating a bootable floppy or a bootable CD-ROM. Create one or the other – or both!

Once you have created a bootable CD or floppy, put it in the appropriate drive, boot your PC to it and follow the instructions on screen to test your system RAM – this will probably take around five minutes, though the time taken will vary according to the speed of your PC and the amount of memory to be checked.

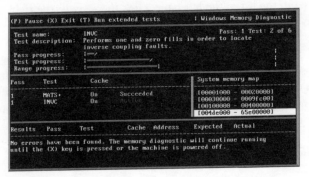

When you have finished, don't forget to remove the bootable disk from the drive before restarting your PC.

MSCONFIG – THE SYSTEM CONFIGURATION UTILITY

This is a diagnostic utility which has been present in all recent Windows. To start it in either version of XP, type MSCONFIG in a Run box or, in Vista, run it from a command line prompt or the Start Search box. You need Administrator rights to do this.

Many of the capabilities of MSCONFIG are beyond the needs of the home user. However, the Startup tab gives you control over which programs run at boot time.

Entries in the list which have a checked box next to them will run at boot time – those which are cleared will not. In this example, two items have been disabled. These programs are still available for use, of course, but will not run automatically at boot time. There are also buttons to enable or disable all startup options.

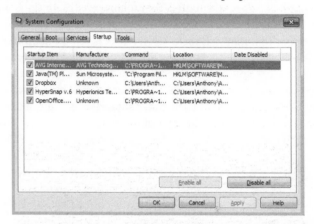

If you want to explore the possibilities of MSCONFIG further, clicking on the **Help** button will take you to an online manual for this utility. There is also a search feature within the Help system which will help you to find the information you need.

USING SAFE MODE

Safe Mode is a diagnostic mode of operation for Windows which has a minimal set of software drivers. Using Safe Mode is described in Chapter 1.

Third-party tools

In addition to the tools provided with Windows there are third-party utilities which are frequently used by system builders and field engineers. One of the best known of these is PC-Check from Eurosoft. This is a fairly expensive (but good) professional tool. Other proprietary diagnostic software utilities are available.

Table 14.1 Common symptoms and solutions

Symptom	Probable cause/solution
System loses time and date settings	Weak or dead CMOS battery. Fit a new battery and update CMOS settings as needed.
Won't boot to floppy or CD-ROM	Check that the disk is in fact bootable – floppies in particular, easily become corrupted or damaged. Check physical connections – data and power cables. Check the 'boot order' using the CMOS 'Setup' utility.
Keyboard errors	Check physical connection to the PC. Check for stuck keys. Check that you have the correct keyboard. See Regional and Language Settings, page 53.
Intermittent boot failures	These are usually caused by: A failing power supply unit. See Replacing a power supply unit, page 106. A virus. Run a virus check, see Chapter 16.
System starts, runs for few minutes, then crashes again.	Typical of an overheating problem. Power down, open the case and check that all fans work when you power up. Check for excessive build-up of dust on heat sinks.
Memory errors	Power down and open the case. Reseat RAM modules. Reboot. If the problem persists run memory diagnostics and replace any RAM found to be faulty.
Won't read a drive	Check cabling and power. Check for presence of removable media in the case of CD/DVD or tape. Test with known good media. Check CMOS settings. Test the drive in another machine. For parallel ATA drives check master/slave jumper settings.

Display problems	Usually caused by wrong settings. Check the Display settings, in the Control Panel. You may need to boot to Safe Mode to do this if the display is unreadable.
Sound/speakers	Check cable connections. Check volume settings in both hardware and software. Look in Device Manager for resource conflicts/driver problems.
Modems	Check cable connections. Check passwords and user names. Check that the phone line is working.

Some common problems and their solutions

Most hardware errors are caused either by failure of a component or by some type of connection problem. Before trying anything else, open the PC case, remove and reseat the suspect component and check that, where necessary, it has power and that any data cable or connector is correctly fitted. Reboot the PC. This is frequently sufficient to cure a problem.

When you have ruled out this sort of simple connectivity problem, remove the component and, if possible, try it in another PC if you have access to one. If it doesn't work in another PC, chances are that it is dead and needs to be replaced. Alternatively, try a new component of the correct type in your PC. For a really cheap item, such as a floppy drive, the cost of simply buying a new component in order to do this is minimal.

Most software or operating system problems are caused by wrong settings or a virus attack.

Table 14.1 is not an exhaustive list, just an indication of some of the most frequently encountered PC problems. Some viruses will mimic hardware failures, so if the PC is functioning sufficiently well a virus scan may be a good first step in the troubleshooting process.

THINGS TO REMEMBER

1 *Device Manager provides an overview of the system and a selection of tools to try to fix them.*

2 *The key to successful troubleshooting is a systematic approach:*
  - ▶ *Describe the problem*
  - ▶ *Reproduce the problem*
  - ▶ *Ask 'What has changed recently?'*

3 *Don't give up. Every time you 'fail' to fix a problem you have eliminated another possibility, i.e. you are step nearer to fixing it.*

4 *Don't forget to check the obvious. For example, power and data connections should be checked and reseated before you embark on anything more complex.*

5 *Don't be afraid to have a go. If all else fails you can use System Restore to roll back your system to an earlier state.*

15

....

The internet and e-mail

In this chapter you will learn:
- *how to set up your Internet connection*
- *how to configure your web browser*
- *how firewalls work*
- *how e-mail works*

How to set up your Internet connection

Connecting to the Internet – for surfing, shopping, online banking, sending and receiving e-mails – is one of the main uses for the Home PC.

BEFORE YOU START

In order to connect to the Internet you need some form of access account with an Internet Service Provider (ISP) and a physical connection through a modem or a router. To set up your Internet connection you will need an active account with your ISP, who will have provided you with a user name and a password – make sure you have these to hand.

Many ISPs provide a broadband modem as part of their broadband package. If this is the case, check that you have all the necessary cables and connectors and that you have read any installation instructions that come with it.

If you have bought your own modem (or router) you should also check any documentation that came with it. This chapter will take you through the setup process for equipment of this type though details may vary between specific products.

SETTINGS AND EQUIPMENT CHECK

As with all equipment installation you should check that you have all necessary cables and connectors and that you have read any instructions from the manufacturer. You will need to know some settings which will be provided by your ISP. These are:

▶ *User name: yourusername@yourisp*
▶ *Password: nnnnnnn.*

(These are needed for all connections including dial-up)

Other settings you may need for your router/broadband modem.

▶ *Encapsulation: PPPoA*
▶ *Multiplexing: VC Based*
▶ *VPI: 0*
▶ *VCI: 38.*

(Note: these are UK settings – if you are not in the UK, they may be different in your country/region.)

You don't need to know what these settings mean – just have them to hand and enter them when – or if – necessary.

Unless you live in a remote area where broadband connection is not available – increasingly uncommon in the UK – you will only need to establish a dialup connection as an emergency measure. If all else fails you can at least access your e-mail, but most websites these days assume that you have a broadband connection and will run very slowly on a dialup connection.

Setting up a dialup connection

Dialup connections are slow, but almost universally available. Unlike a broadband connection which is tied to a phone line, a typical pay-as-you-go dialup service can generally be accessed from any phone line and is billed to the telephone account. Some people also like to have a dialup available as a fall-back service if there are problems with their ADSL connection. A dial-up connection requires you to have a modem installed on your system. Built-in dialup modems are not as common on new systems as they used to be so you may need to install either an internal or an external modem on your system.

PHYSICAL CONNECTION

If you don't have a modem port on your PC you will need to fit one, either as a PCI expansion card or as an external USB or serial port device. Chapter 7 outlines how to fit a PCI card and USB is covered later in this chapter. The example that follows shows the process of installing an external serial port modem. The advantage – as you will see – is that even without drivers you can still set up a basic connection.

1 *Attach the modem to the phone plug on the wall and connect it to the serial port on the back of the PC (this is 9-pin male port). Turn on the power to the modem. There is no need to reboot the PC.*

2 *Navigate to the Phone and Modem section of the Control Panel (the quick way is to search on 'modem') and click on the* **Add** *button. This will start the Add Hardware Wizard. Make sure that your modem is turned on before you continue.*

3 *Click on* **Next** *to see if the modem will Plug and Play. If it does just follow the instructions on the screen and be ready to provide drivers from disk if you are prompted to do so. If the*

modem is unrecognized and you don't have any drivers for it, here is the workround:

4 *Select the Choose From a List option. You will see a list like this. Choose the modem that is closest to the one that you have then click on* **Next** *to continue.*

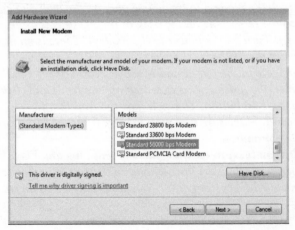

5 *Highlight the port where you want to install the modem (COM 1 in the figure is the first serial port>).and click on the* **Next** *button. Windows will now install the modem. With the modem physically attached and installed the next job is to configure it to attach to the Internet.*

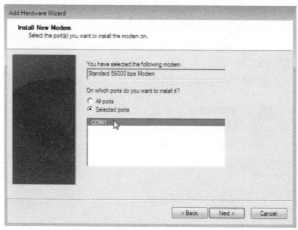

6 *Search Control Panel for Modem and select Set Up a Dial-up Connection. This starts a form-fill dialog box for you to enter the required information.*

7 *When you have finished entering information, click on **Next** and Windows will start the connection. If it fails, check all physical connections and go back and check the accuracy of the information that you have supplied and try again.*

Once the modem has been set up it becomes available through the connection icon in the System Tray.

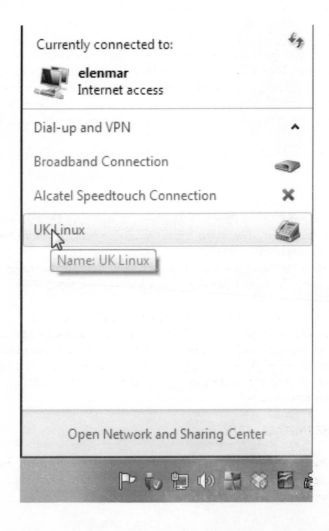

> Setting up a Standard modem with no drivers will mean
> losing any advanced features of the device – such as voice
> or fax services. However, it is a better than nothing solution
> even if you only use it to order a new broadband router!

Installing a USB broadband modem

The most popular way of connecting to the Internet is through
some form of broadband connection – this is also known as an
Asymmetric Digital Subscriber Line (ADSL) connection. As we will
see in Chapter 17, this type of modem connection can be shared over
a home network. For the time being, however, we will look at the
process of installing a fairly typical broadband modem for a single PC.

The modem used in this example is a cheap generic one based on a
chip set from Lucent Technologies.

BEFORE YOU START

1 *Unpack the modem and check the cables and connectors are
   all present and correct.*
2 *Make sure that you have all connection details provided by
   your ISP to hand (see the section Settings and Equipment
   Check above).*
3 *Check that you have the manufacturer's driver CD.*
4 *Read any documentation. In this instance, for example, you are
   warned not to allow Windows to Plug and Play the new modem
   but to insert the driver CD and install the manufacturer's drivers.*
5 *Don't plug the modem into the USB port yet. You will be
   prompted later.*

THE INSTALLATION

1 *Put the driver CD in the CD/DVD drive and navigate to the
   setup program for your system. NB: Do not let it autorun
   when Windows detects it.*

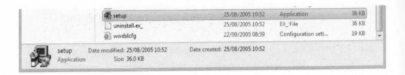

2 *Click on the setup.exe file to run it. Skip over the Unknown Publisher warning from Windows.*

3 *Accept the Licence Agreement and click on **Next** until you reach the Communication Settings page.*

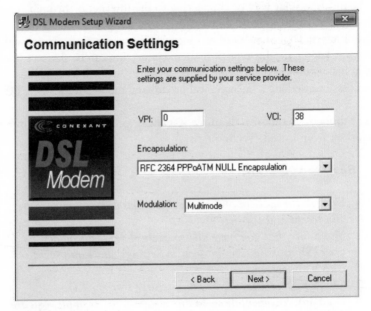

4 *Enter the communications settings provided by your ISP then click on **Next**. After a final check that the settings are correct click on **Next** again to start the installation of the drivers.*

5 *As the installation proceeds you will receive another Unknown Publisher warning from Windows. Choose the Install Anyway option. You will be prompted to plug the modem into the USB port. Connect the modem and click on **Next**.*

6 *When the installer prompts you to reboot, click on the **Close** button.*

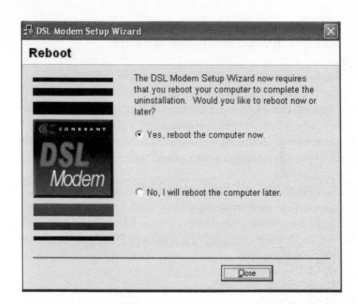

7 *After the reboot, click on the connection icon and enter your user name and password to access your broadband account.*

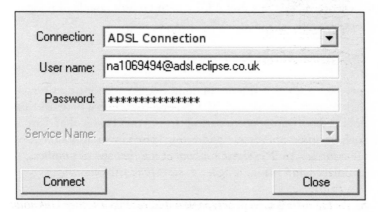

In this example we have walked through the installation of a 'typical' ADSL modem. Your modem will probably be different in some of its details so read the supplier's documentation before you start.

Installing a broadband modem/router

An increasingly popular way of connecting to the Internet is through a combined broadband modem/router. These are standalone devices which are permanently connected to the Internet even when your PC is turned off. They often provide wireless network connectivity as well, and are ideal for use with a small home network – whether wired, wireless, or both.

The example that follows assumes that you have a working Ethernet port on your machine – most modern machines do. If you don't have a network connection – for an RJ45 plug or a wireless card – you will need to install one. Fitting a PCI Expansion card is described in Chapter 8.

In this chapter we will look at how to set up a modem/router through the browser on a single PC and return to the networking aspects in Chapter 17.

In order to do this, it's useful for you to know a couple of things about network addresses.

NETWORK ADDRESSES

A network address is a series of numbers, like a phone number, which identifies a node such as a PC or a router on a network. The rules for these numbers are part of the Internet Protocol and are known as Internet Protocol addresses. This is invariably shortened to IP address. An IP address consists of four groups of numbers, separated by full stops.

192.168.2.1 – is a typical private IP address. Private addresses are reserved for use on private networks – like home networks – rather than the public addresses used on the (public) Internet.

Just as a phone number may consist of an exchange code and the individual's phone number, an IP address has two parts. In the case of a typical Class C address that you will use for home networking, the first three groups of numbers are the network part of the address and the last group indicates the computer, or router, or other device attached to that network. The address 192.168.2.1, then indicates device number 1 on the network indicated by 192.168.2.

BEFORE YOU START

Check that you have all equipment and documentation (as in previous examples). You will also need to know the router's default IP address and its default user name and password. This information will be in its manual or setup instructions The default IP address in this example is 192.168.2.1 – this may be different if you are using a different make or model of router/modem.

CONNECTING YOUR ROUTER

1 *Connect all cables. There will be one from the Ethernet port on your PC to one of the ports on the router, and another from the router to the splitter which connects it and the phone to the phone line. Connect the router to its power supply. Various lights on the router will flicker as it runs through its power-on self-test/boot sequence.*

2 *When the router has settled down you will have an indicator to show that it is powered up along with other indicators for the ADSL side of the connection. The port to which you have connected the Ethernet cable should have a steady light to show that it is in place. Ports which have no cable attached will not show lights. If there are any problems at this stage – unlikely – then check cable connections and power and have a look at the router manual or setup instructions.*

3 *The next thing to do is to configure the modem/router through its web interface. To do this, start your web browser and type in the default IP address of your router. You don't need 'http' or 'www' – just type the numeric IP address in the Address bar and press [Enter].*

4 *The browser will add the http:// prefix for you and you will be taken to the login screen for the router. As this is the first time you have accessed the router there won't be a password in place – or if there is, it will be a default password from the manufacturer which will be shown in the documentation. The login screen will look something like this:*

5 *Enter a password – if necessary – and press [Enter]. The Welcome screen will list various options, including a setup wizard. You can use the wizard to enter the necessary information to set up your connection. For purposes of this example we will walk through the stages manually.*

6 *The first page to complete is Basic Settings:*

Here you need to enter:
   ▷ *Encapsulation method. Choose from the drop-down list.*
   ▷ *Your login/user name – provided by your ISP*
   ▷ *Your password – probably provided by your ISP to begin with but which you can later change through their site.*

Unless you have good reason to do so you should leave the other options at their default values. When you have checked the accuracy of the information click on the **Apply** *button at the bottom of the screen. Don't bother with the* **Test** *button yet; this is a new set up and there is more information to be entered – the ADSL settings required by your ISP.*

7 *Click on the ADSL entry in the menu then enter the information supplied by your ISP in the fields on the form.*

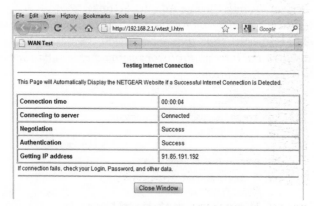

Click on the **Apply** *button when your are finished.*

8 *Return to the Basic Setting page (see step 6) and click on the* **Test** *button. Initially this may report a failure but after a few seconds (if you have entered all the information correctly) it will report success.*

9 *Click on the* **Close Window** *button. The router will need to reboot in order to save your settings – this may take half a minute or so.*

10 *In order to test your router, point your browser at a website and check that it loads okay.*

11 *This may be a good time to go back to the configuration utility and check other system settings – these will include some options such as blocking PING requests from the Internet which we will consider later when we look at firewalls or enabling/disabling wireless access which we will consider in Chapter 18. The only setting that you really need to fix now is the password to access the router configuration screens – the default password for popular routers is easily available on the Internet so it is sensible to choose something of your own.*

IF YOUR BROWSER WON'T CONNECT

If your browser can't see the router, then it is probably a problem with the network settings on your PC. Navigate to **Control Panel > Troubleshooting > Network and Internet** and run the **Internet Connections Troubleshooter Wizard**. If this doesn't come up with a solution you can troubleshoot the problem manually.

1 *Navigate to* **Control Panel > Network and Internet > Network and Sharing Center.**
2 *Click on the link* **Change Adapter Settings.**
3 *Right-click on the icon for the Local Area Connection and select* **Properties** *from the context menu.*
4 *Highlight the Internet Protocol version 4 entry and click on the Properties button.*

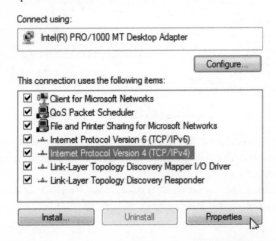

5 *Make sure – in the Properties screen – that your system is set up to obtain an IP address and DNS server address automatically.*

How to configure your web browser

Most home users use the Microsoft Internet Explorer web browser which is supplied with the Windows operating system. Most of the default values are suitable for most users, though there are a couple of entries that you may want to change.

1 *Open Internet Explorer, select Tools from the menu at the top right of the screen then select Internet Options from the bottom of the drop-down list.*

2 *The* **General** *tab has most of the setting that are likely to be of use or interest to the home user. The top section allows you to change your home page – where the browser starts when it opens. The easy way to change this is to go to the Internet page that you want to use as 'home', then click* **Use Current.**

3 *The next section – Browsing History – provides a* **Delete** *button so that you can remove all your browsing history and a checkbox so that you can automatically delete your browsing history every time you close the browser. There's also a* **Settings** *button which allows you to fine-tune your settings for both history and stored web pages (the web cache).*

4 *The* **Search Settings** *section allows you to change the default search engine that powers the search box at the top right of Internet Explorer. The default is Microsoft's own Bing engine. To change this use the drop-down list in the search box in Internet Explorer and select* **Find More Providers.** *When you have done this and selected (say) Google you can make this the default by returning to the* **Search Settings** *button under the* **General** *tab.*

5 *The* **Tabs** *section allows you to decide how tabbed browsing is implemented.*

6 *The bottom section –* **Appearance** *– gives you the opportunity to change colours, fonts, etc., though for most users the defaults are satisfactory.*

How firewalls work

When you connect to the Internet you are starting a two-way communication process. When you click on a link or type a web address in a browser bar you are requesting information to be sent to you. Unfortunately, there is nothing to stop anyone from sending you material that you have not requested. There are malicious programs which will invade your system for purposes such as data or identity theft or simply to damage your system for the sake of it.

In order to counter these threats you can use a firewall. This may be implemented in hardware or in software.

> One of the advantages of using a router rather than a modem – including ADSL Broadband modems – is that a router by its nature acts as a firewall by using Network Address Translation.

Whatever the specifics of your firewall, its basic function is that of a doorkeeper examining invitations – no invitation, no entry. When you request a page from the Internet it passes through the firewall which notes the request. When the remote site replies, the data packets which it sends are compared with the firewall's table of requests sent, and are only allowed in if they have been specifically requested by you. By default, any Windows 7 PC will have this level of firewall protection implemented.

THE WINDOWS FIREWALL

An additional level of protection is given by controlling which programs on your PC can access the Internet. Obviously, your web browser and e-mail programs need to be given access. Other programs can be given access to the Internet if you allow them.

The screenshot shows a program attempting to access the Internet and being intercepted by the Windows firewall. If you wish to give this program access, click on the **Allow Access** button. Choosing the **Cancel** button will leave it blocked. In order to check or modify access through the Windows firewall navigate to **Control Panel > System and Security > Windows firewall > Allow a program .....** You will see a list of programs like this:

By default this is a read-only list. If you want to change the settings of a program you need to click on the **Change Settings** button before changing the checkbox(es) next to the program in the list.

If you have a home network, by the way, you only need to set up a firewall on the machine which has the direct Internet connection. Other machines which connect through this 'gateway' machine are protected by its firewall. This does not apply to virus protection. Each PC should have its own anti-virus software package which should be regularly updated.

TESTING YOUR FIREWALL

Your firewall should close all ports on your PC so that they cannot be seen from the Internet. A very good – and free – service is from the Gibson Research Corporation at www.grc.com. Their Shields Up utility will remotely probe your PC and report any security holes which they detect. This site is also a good source of general Internet security information.

How e-mail works

E-mail is one of the most widely used features of the Internet. We generally take it for granted these days that we can communicate more or less instantly with anyone in the world through e-mail. For the home user, there are two e-mail types – web-based services or POP3 services with addresses like yourname@yourisp.com.

Web-based services require you to log on to a site where you have an e-mail account and everything is done whilst logged on to that site. Probably the best known web-based mail service is Microsoft's Hotmail, though there are many alternative services such gmx.com or fastmail.fm.

POP3 services allow you to use a mail program such Windows Live Mail or Thunderbird. These are all programs – known as mail clients – which allow you to compose mail off-line, then connect to the Internet to send your messages and download any that you have received. This is the mail type which is most widely used by anyone who has to deal with more than a handful of mail messages per day, though you can of course have both types of e-mail account. Windows Live Mail supports both POP3 and its own Hotmail service in one application.

Sending and receiving POP3 e-mails means using two e-mail protocols – the Post Office Protocol – version 3 (POP3), which is used for receiving e-mails and the Simple Mail Transfer Protocol (SMTP), which is used for sending messages from your PC. In order to set up your e-mail client, you don't need to know anything about these mail protocols other than their names. What you do need to know, of course, is the names and addresses of the servers that use these protocols, along with your user name and password.

Chapter 4, has a section under the heading *Gathering the Information*, which looks at how to find (or enter) the e-mail settings needed to make your e-mail system work. The illustrations are of the Windows Live Mail client as this is the most popular e-mail program with home users. It is not, however, difficult to apply the information given to other mail client programs. Just remember that you need two server addresses – possibly with the same password for each – a POP3 server for receiving incoming mail and an SMTP server for sending mail.

THINGS TO REMEMBER

1 *Before setting up your Internet connection make sure that you
have all the necessary settings from your ISP.*

2 *Always check cabling and connectors for hardware before you
start.*

3 *If you are installing a modem – dial-up or ADSL – make
sure that you have the necessary drivers. If you don't have
an installation CD you may need to visit the manufacturer's
website (possibly on a different machine) and download them.*

4 *A router has a built-in firewall and is therefore more secure
than using a modem connection.*

5 *The Windows firewall will block all new programs by default
unless you decide otherwise.*

6 *You can change your Windows firewall settings and program
access through the Control Panel.*

7 *A firewall does NOT protect you against viruses. You will
need a separate virus scanner. Chapter 16 covers viruses and
malware.*

16

Viruses and other malware

In this chapter you will learn:
- *how to combat viruses and other malware*
- *about InPrivate browsing*
- *how to set up parental control on Internet access*
- *how to deal with a virus infection*

Viruses, trojans and worms

If you believed all the stories you hear about the various threats that lurk on the Internet you would probably never go online again! The truth of the matter is, however, a bit less dramatic. There are some nasties around, but some sensible precautions are enough to make the risks manageable.

Viruses, trojans and worms are all types of malicious program code written with the intention of damaging some aspect of your PC's operation. They are often referred to collectively as malware. There are also other types of malicious code – diallers, browser hijackers, etc. – and the differences between the various nasties is not always clear, but the kind of people who write malicious code are unlikely to care too much about definitions.

Basic precautions

To keep your PC safe from attack you should download and install any security updates from Microsoft. Don't forget that if you have reinstalled Windows you will have lost all your accumulated security downloads and will have to download and install them again.

You also need a firewall of some kind. The minimum precaution is to use the Windows firewall that was bundled with Service Pack 2. If you are using a combined broadband modem/router this may also have a firewall built into it. Make sure that it is enabled. A firewall will provide basic protection from worms – such as Sasser or Netsky – which circulate on the Internet looking for vulnerable systems to exploit.

INSTALLING AND USING ANTI-VIRUS SOFTWARE

The single most important tool for dealing with virus threats is an anti-virus software package. This needs to be installed and regularly updated. Most packages can be configured to update themselves regularly and this may happen a couple of times a week. An out-of-date virus scanner is worse than useless – it will not protect you from the ever-evolving pool of viruses but will make you think that you are protected when you are not!

There are many anti-virus packages available and they have many similarities with each other. One of the most effective and easy to use is AVG from Grisoft. They offer a number of packages for various sizes and types of business – more importantly for the home user, they offer a free version for private use. Check that you are eligible to use the free version – if you are a private household wishing to protect a single PC you almost certainly are – then download and install the free package. If you are not eligible to use the free version – you have more than one PC or your PC is attached to a network – you should visit www.grisoft.com and check on the licensing of their paid-for products and trial versions. You can also download a reference guide and an installation guide from their site.

To find out more about AVG Free Edition and AVG Trial Versions visit http://free.grisoft.com.

Installing the anti-virus package – whether AVG or other – is no different from installing any other piece of software on your system. Make sure that you have sufficient rights – you'll need Administrator rights – and click on the installer file icon to start the process. Follow the on-screen instructions until the installer has finished running – you may have to reboot the system at some point. The example which follows is of AVG Free edition – illustrations by courtesy of Grisoft sro, Czech Republic.

INSTALLING AVG FREE EDITION

1   *The AVG installer has the company logo on its icon. In order to install AVG you will need Administrator privileges, so right-click on the installer icon and select* **Run as Administrator** *from the context menu.*

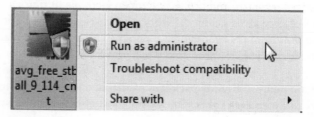

2   *Skip over the security warning from Windows, choose your language from the drop-down menu (the default is English) then click on the* **Next** *button to proceed. You will be presented with at choice to install either the free product or a trial version of the full product. Make your choice and click on the appropriate link, then on the* **Next** *button. (For purposes of this example this will be the free version). The installer will now spend a couple of minutes downloading the installation files.*

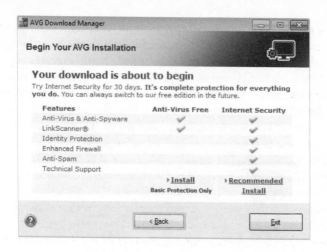

3 Read the Licence Agreement, tick the box to say that you have done this, then click on the **Accept** button to proceed.

4 At the next screen you will be given the choice between a *Standard installation (the default)* or *Custom installation*. Choose the *Standard installation* and click on **Next**. At the next screen, confirm your user name and accept the assigned licence number, then click on **Next**.

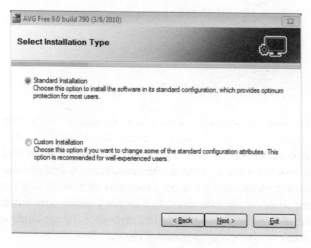

5 *You will now be given the opportunity to install some optional extras. Make your selection(s) and click on the* **Next** *button to proceed. The installer will now spend several minutes copying files and configuring your system. There is a* **Cancel** *button if you change your mind but apart from this there is nothing for you to do but watch until the Installer confirms that it has finished. When this happens, click on the* **Finish** *button.*

6 *With the installation complete the next stage is to Optimize Scanning Performance. This can be deferred if you wish, but for purposes of this worked example we will click on the recommended* **Optimize scanning now** *option. This may take several minutes; the exact length of time depends, of course, on your particular hardware resources.*

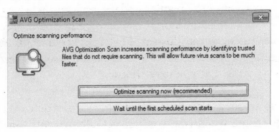

7 *Once the initial scan is complete, click on the System Tray icon to open the AVG user interface. It should confirm that all AVG components are up-to-date and working.
Just to be on the safe side, click on the* **Update now** *button and if there are any updates available click on the* **Update** *button to download and install them.*

8 *Now that you have a fully working up to date virus scanner, click on the* **Computer scanner** *button to start a whole system scan. This will take several minutes – longer if you have a lot of files. With luck, you will receive an all clear message. If not, follow the instructions on screen and/or look at the section How to Deal With a Virus Infection later in the chapter.*

Scheduling updates and scans

Whatever anti-virus package you have installed, you need to consider how to organize regular updates and system scans that fit in with your pattern of PC use and your type of Internet connection. Again, this is illustrated by reference to AVG Free, though similar procedures should be available in any other anti-virus package that you may choose.

If you have an always-on broadband connection you can schedule updates for times when you won't be actually working on the PC, with a system scan scheduled to run after any update.

SCHEDULING UPDATES

1 *Open the AVG interface by clicking on its icon in the System Tray then click on the* **Overview** *button from the menu on the left.*

2 *Click on the Update Manager icon (bottom right).*

3 *You can choose to Update Now. More importantly for our present purposes you can specify the time of day and frequency of updates. Make your choices and click on the* **Save changes** *button.*

SCHEDULING SCANS

1 *Open the AVG interface by clicking on its icon in the System Tray then click on the* **Computer scanner** *button from the menu on the left.*
2 *Click on the* **Schedule Scans** *icon (bottom right).*
3 *Click on the* **Edit scan schedule** *button and make your choices:*

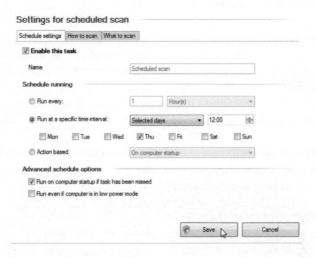

4 *Click on* **Save** *to save your new settings then exit from the AVG interface.*

It's a good idea to schedule you updates so that they run just before your scans so that you can be sure that you are scanning with the latest virus definition files.

Windows Defender

Windows Defender is part of Windows 7 but it is not turned on by default when Windows is installed. You need to turn it on and to configure it.

1 *To turn Defender on, search on 'defender' in the Search box on the* **Start** *menu and select Windows Defender from the resulting list. You will see a notification like this. Click on the link to start Defender.*

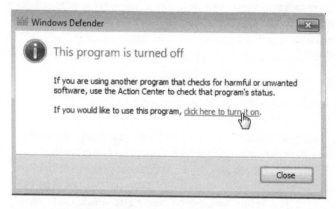

2 *Click on the Scan tool to run a quick scan.*

3 *Choose* **Tools** *from the main menu, then* **Options**. *You can now schedule scans and default actions for Defender. These settings are similar to those for your virus scanner. Unless you disable it, Windows Defender will now start whenever you boot to Windows and will run in the background to protect you from malware.*

> Defender is NOT a virus scanner. It is bad practice to run more than one virus scanner on a system at the same time as they may clash and each may 'detect' the other as a virus. This is not the case with Defender which complements and works with your virus scanner.

OTHER SPYWARE AND AD-WARE DETECTION PACKAGES

Windows Defender is not the only tool available for spyware and ad-ware detection and removal. There are several other packages – such as Lavasoft's AdAware or Spybot Search and Destroy which can be downloaded free for personal use.

SmartScreen Filter in Internet Explorer 8

Phishing (pronounced 'fishing') is the increasingly common practice of sending e-mails which appear to come from a reputable source such as your bank, asking you to confirm contact details, login information or even passwords. The best way to avoid trouble is simply to delete any suspicious e-mails. However, as an extra layer of precaution, Internet Explorer 8 ships with SmartScreen Filter to combat phishing attacks. Like Defender this is not turned on by default at install time. In order to fix this:

1 *Start Internet Explorer.*
2 *Click on the* **Safety** *button (top right).*

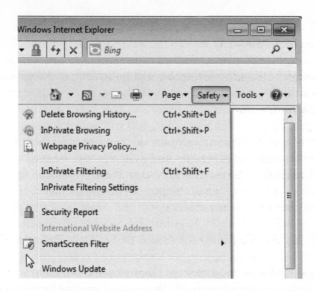

3 *Click on the* **SmartScreen Filter** *entry in the drop-down menu.*
4 *Now that it is activated SmartScreen Filter will:*
  ▷ *Check websites against a list of reported phishing and malware sites.*
  ▷ *Check software downloads against a list of reported malware sites.*
  ▷ *Warn you if you visit known phishing websites and other websites that may contain malware that may lead to identity theft.*
5 *If there is a problem with a site you will see a warning like this:*

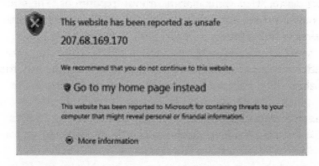

InPrivate browsing

This is another security feature built in to Internet Explorer 8.

Normally, when you visit a website Explorer keeps a record of where you have been (a history list) and will accept cookies from sites so that they can identify you when you return to them. Some sites contain links to other sites and these too may be tracked usually for legitimate reasons. However, there are times – such as when you are using a public computer – when you don't want this information to be recorded and stored. InPrivate browsing gives you the option to turn off these features for the current session ONLY. To activate the service choose the InPrivate Filtering entry from the Safety menu in Internet Explorer or press [Control] + [Shift] + [F]. When you exit from the browser session you will have left no trail of your activities for that session and the browser will resume its earlier settings next time it is started.

Parental control software

There is no censorship on the World Wide Web – no one owns it or controls it – and for the most part that is beneficial to all of us. However, it does mean that there are some pretty unpleasant websites varying from the salacious to the downright perverted and no matter what we may think about freedom of expression for adults most people agree that children should be protected from undesirable web content.

As with spyware and ad-ware, public perception of the problems of pornography, violence or racism on the Net, has led to the development of software tools to deal with the problems, and to restrict access to sites which you regard as unsuitable. Parental control software has been available as a third-party add-on for several years. These tend to be reasonably priced rather than free. Two of the best known of these are Net Nanny and Cyber

Sentinel. These can be bought on disk from some retail outlets or downloaded from the Internet.

The Parental Controls in Windows 7 are sufficient for most users. You can set them up through the Control Panel (search on the keyword 'parental') or turn back to Chapter 3 to refresh your memory of how they work.

How to deal with a virus infection

If you think that you have a virus infection the first thing to do is to scan your system with an up-to-date virus scanner. If you don't have a scanner, or it is out of date, then install one and obtain any necessary updates for it before you do anything else.

If your system won't boot at all, this could be a problem with hardware (try reseating power and data cables on the disk itself) or, if the system boots only sporadically, the problem may be a failing power supply unit (PSU). Check the PSU with a multimeter and replace it if its outputs are less than 12 volts on the Yellow lines and 5 volts on the red lines. If you have ruled out the possibility of hardware failure then failure to boot may be the result of a boot sector/partition sector virus. The cure for this is simple: boot to a repair disk and install a new boot sector on the hard drive.

We looked at how to make a repair disk in Chapter 2 and you should have one somewhere. If you don't have one then you can make one on someone else's system because they are interchangeable, the only limitation being that you need a 32-bit disk for a 32-bit system and a 64-bit disk for a 64-bit system.

USING A REPAIR DISK TO FIX A BOOT SECTOR VIRUS

1 *Put the repair disk in the CD/DVD drive and boot the system to it. This may take a couple of minutes.*

2 *Set the keyboard language to suit your location from the first graphical menu then click on the Next button. The repair disk will now scan your system and identify any installed version of Windows 7. For most users there will only be one installed version.*

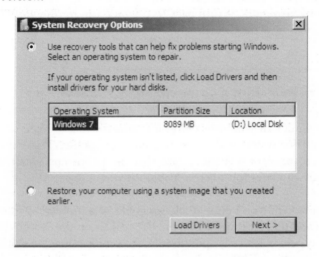

3 *Make a note of the drive letter where Windows 7 is installed, then click on Next.*

4 *At the next screen you will be presented with a menu. Choose the last item in the list – Command Prompt – and click on the link to launch the Command Line processor.*

5 *At the command prompt issue the command:*

BOOTSECT /NT60 D: [CR]

6 *The system will confirm the repair.*

7 *Reboot and remove the repair disk and store it somewhere safe.*

Note that the final element in the command line is the drive letter that you noted at step 2 above. Your drive letter may be different. Note, too, the importance of spaces in the command line. If you read it out loud it is: BOOTSECT [SPACE] /NT60 [SPACE] YOURDRIVELETTER: (The capital letters are used for clarity – the command line prompt is not case-sensitive).

CLEANING UP

Just because you have fixed the boot sector virus that was the immediate problem it doesn't mean to say that there aren't other copies or other viruses elsewhere on your hard disk or floppies. There are three things that you need to check thoroughly:

▶ **Your hard disk(s)** – *do a full scan with an up-to-date virus scanner. It is a good idea to disable System Restore while scanning so that the scanner can search and destroy anything hiding in the protected system area. You will lose any system restore points, but it's a price worth paying for an effective full scan. Don't forget to turn it on when you have finished!*
▶ **Floppy disks and pen drives** – *scan and mark with a pen or sticky label every floppy disk and pen drive that you have. Make sure you check any disks that belong to other family members.*
▶ **Scan backups and archives** – *you may have backed up the virus before you realized it was present. If you discover a virus that you have accidentally backed up to a CD or DVD and it is a rewritable disk then you can reformat it. Otherwise, damage it to make it unreadable (a knife blade will do this quite well!) before you throw it away.*

Some viruses require you to download a specific cleanup program. Most of the major anti-virus companies maintain a list of current 'top threats' on their websites and make cleanup programs available for particular known pests.

THINGS TO REMEMBER

1 *An out-of-date virus scanner is worse than useless. Keep your scanner up to date.*

2 *Schedule updates to the scanner so that they are automatically downloaded and applied.*

3 *Schedule a regular virus scan. Set this to run soon after the update.*

4 *Windows Defender is not turned on by default. Turn it on to protect yourself from malware.*

5 *Familiarize yourself with Internet Explorer features such as SmartScreen Filter and InPrivate Browsing.*

6 *There must be a standard (non-administrative) user account on the PC if you want to implement Parental Controls.*

7 *You can use a Windows 7 repair disk made on another system to restore your boot sector after a boot sector/partition sector virus infection.*

8 *After you have fixed a virus infection you need to clean up all possible sources of reinfection such as removable drives.*

17

Home networking

In this chapter you will learn:
- *how to set up a small network*
- *how to share files, printers and an Internet connection over a network*
- *about cloud storage*

Networking with Windows 7

Windows 7 has radically changed the way that we go about the business of home networking. Connecting two or more PCs to share files and resources can be achieved by creating a HomeGroup on one of your PCs then inviting other systems to join it. The whole operation is controlled through Control Panel > Network and Internet > HomeGroup. You can access this through the Control Panel or by searching on 'HomeGroup' from the Start menu.

> Legacy systems – Vista and XP – and legacy technologies such as sharing a modem are not compatible with HomeGroup. It is technically possible to connect a Windows 7 machine to an older system but the techniques needed to create a 'mixed' network are beyond the scope of this book.

Hardware

Obviously there has to be a physical connection between the PCs (even wireless is considered to be 'physical' in this context) though the most popular method is a wired connection between the PCs and an Ethernet switch/router.

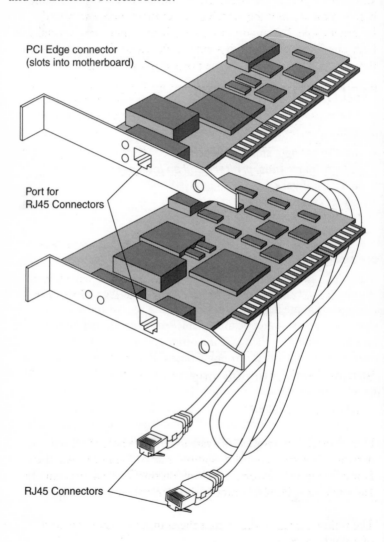

PCI Edge connector
(slots into motherboard)

Port for
RJ45 Connectors

RJ45 Connectors

A PC which is sufficiently modern to run Windows 7 will have an Ethernet port at the back. To establish a physical connection between the PC and the switch connect them with a standard Ethernet cable. When you buy a switch or router there's usually at least one such cable provided with it. Provided that the connectors (known as RJ45s) will fit in the ports it is an Ethernet cable.

Beware of accidentally using a crossover cable by mistake. These are specialist cables designed to link two PCs without a hub or switch. They should be marked as 'Crossover' or 'X-over' but labels sometimes go missing. If in doubt, buy a new straight-through patch cable.

CONNECTING THE HARDWARE

1 *Connect both PCs to the shared switch/router. There's no need to power down to do this.*
2 *Make sure that the switch/router has power. There should be a power indicator light as well as connection lights for each of the ports.*

Setting up the HomeGroup

BEFORE YOU START

HomeGroup only works for systems that are part of a home network. If your Network Location is anything but Home then HomeGroup won't work. To check on this/fix it navigate to the Network and Sharing Center in the Control Panel.

The following figure shows that the computer Asimov is part of a public network.

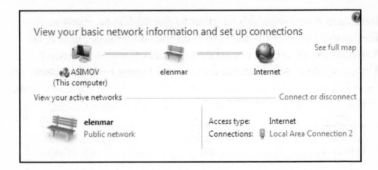

To change this setting click on the **Public Network** link. You will see something like this:

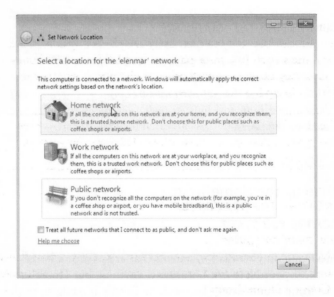

Select **Home Network** to change your location.

THE BASIC SET UP

This example walks through the process of setting up a Home Group in a typical home network situation using two PCs which are connected to a combined Ethernet Switch/Home Router. The 'main' computer is STEINBECK and the 'new' computer is ASIMOV. Both are connected by Ethernet cables to the switch. The initial Network Map (in the Control Panel) looks like this:

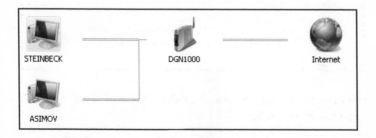

As you can see from the figure, both PCs are connected to the router and can 'see' the Internet. They are physically connected through the switch (the same physical unit as the router) but at this stage they cannot see each other or share resources because the HomeGroup has not yet been set up.

The terms 'main' and 'new' are used here to distinguish the two systems that we are networking. Once the network is set up, they are equal partners in a peer group.

CREATING THE HOMEGROUP

On the 'main' computer

1 *Navigate to HomeGroup – either through the Control Panel or by searching in the Start menu, and click on the button to* **Create a HomeGroup**.

2 *Select which things you want to share (this figure shows the Windows 7 defaults) and click on* **Next**. *Windows will display a progress bar as it works, then present you with a password for the newly created HomeGroup.*

3 *Make a note of (or print) the password for the HomeGroup, then click on the* **Finish** *button.*

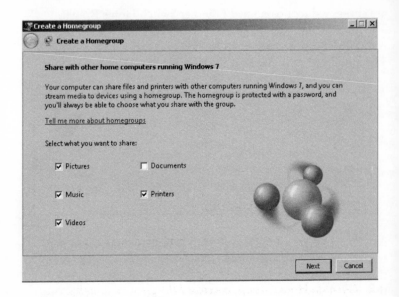

Type the homegroup password

A password helps prevent unauthorized access to homegroup files and printers. You can get the password from the person who set up your homegroup.

Where can I find the homegroup password?

Type the new homegroup password from Anthony:

hH4Gj5kK8J

On the 'new' computer

1 *Navigate to HomeGroup – either through the Control Panel or by searching in the* **Start** *menu. You will see something like:*

2 *Click on the* **Join now** *button to accept the default sharing arrangements – these can be change later once the connection is set up and tested.*

3 *Enter the password when prompted – it is case-sensitive – then click on* **Next**. *Windows will confirm that the new computer is now part of the HomeGroup. Click on* **Finish**.

Change homegroup settings

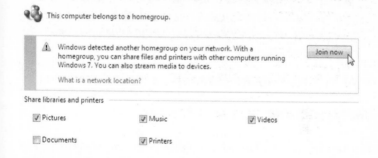

This computer belongs to a homegroup.

⚠ Windows detected another homegroup on your network. With a homegroup, you can share files and printers with other computers running Windows 7. You can also stream media to devices.

[Join now]

What is a network location?

Share libraries and printers

☑ Pictures   ☑ Music   ☑ Videos

☐ Documents   ☑ Printers

VIEWING YOUR HOMEGROUP

1 Click on your name or on the **Computer** entry in the **Start** menu. In the panel on the left you will see an entry for HomeGroup.

2 Click on **HomeGroup** to expand the view. You will see something like this:

3 *The panel on the right shows users who are currently logged on to a computer that is a member of the HomeGroup and who have allowed sharing on some of their files. Clicking on a user's icon will expand the list to show which files and folders are share.*

FINE TUNING YOUR HOMEGROUP – A WORKED EXAMPLE

INSTALLING AND SHARING A PRINTER

When you set up your HomeGroup printer sharing was enabled by default. We now need to connect a printer locally to one PC and then share it across the group.

For purposes of this example we'll use an Epson printer, connected to a USB port. Windows 7 has very good support for USB devices and the popular brands of printer. In this case – an Epson Photo 870 – Windows Plug and Play will do the job. If you have to install drivers from a disk and you need to refresh your memory on this topic go back and look at Chapter 11.

1 *Plug the printer into the USB port and turn on the power. Allow it to Plug and Play.*

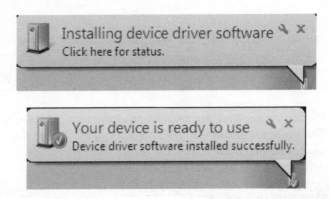

2 *Navigate to* **Control Panel > Hardware and Sound > Devices and Printers**. *As you can see from the figure the newly installed*

printer is already shared because you enabled it (by default) when you set up the HomeGroup.

 EPSON Stylus Photo 890 State: 🖧 Shared
Model: EPSON Stylus Photo 890
Category: Printer

3 *Go to another PC that is a member of the HomeGroup and navigate to* **Control Panel > Hardware and Sound > Devices and Printers.**

4 *Click on the* **Add a printer** *button at the top. Click on the option to Add a Network Printer, then click on* **Next.**

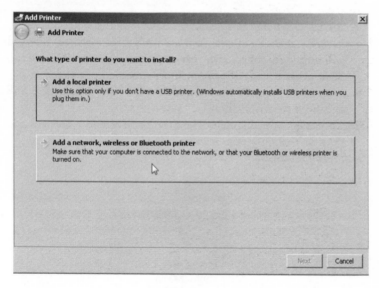

5 *Windows will search for installed printers in your HomeGroup. This may take a couple of minutes to complete. Select the newly installed printer from the list (in this case there's only one). Click on* **Next** *to continue.*

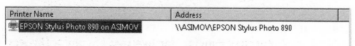

Printer Name	Address
EPSON Stylus Photo 890 on ASIMOV	\\ASIMOV\EPSON Stylus Photo 890

6 *You will now be prompted to install drivers.*

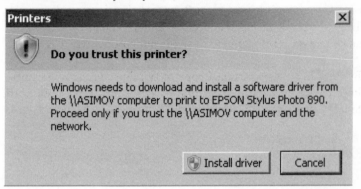

7 *As you know that this printer is something that you have just installed, it is safe to click on the Install Driver option. Windows will install the appropriate drivers for your printer. When this is done, you will have the opportunity to print a test page.*

8 *Print a test page on your newly installed network printer, then exit from the installer.*

9 *Check in* **Control Panel > Hardware and Sound > Devices and Printers** *that your new printer is in place and is (in this case) the default printer.*

EPSON Stylus
Photo 890 on
ASIMOV

Job done!

USING LIBRARIES

Libraries are a new feature in Windows 7. They are not a network feature as such, but they may include files that are physically stored in network locations. At first glance libraries look very much like ordinary Windows folders but they are in fact virtual folders – a set of links to files that are physically stored elsewhere on the system. They provide a means of collecting scattered items that may be anywhere on the system into a single point of access.

By default, a newly installed copy of Windows has four libraries in place. If you click on the Libraries icon – just to the right of the **Start** button – you will see the default Windows libraries.

In order to look at the contents of a library just click on it as you would any other folder.

ADDING A LIBRARY

To create a new library click on the **New library** button on the top menu. This will create a new Library (virtual folder) which you can rename to something more meaningful than its default title of New Library – in this case the name is Book Files.

To share the new library, right-click on its icon and select from the context menu.

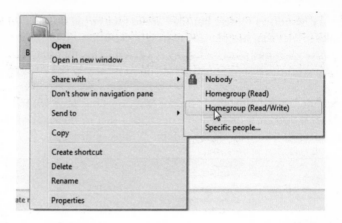

As you can see, you can share – Read Only or Read/Write – with other users and members of your HomeGroup. As long as the machine that holds the shared files is available – i.e. is turned on and participating in the HomeGroup then the files that you have shared will be available with whatever rights you have assigned to them.

ADDING FILES TO YOUR LIBRARY

1 *Right-click on the library icon and choose either Properties or Open in a new window from the context menu. You will see something like this:*

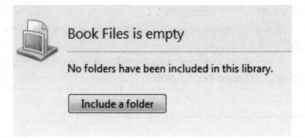

2 *Click on the* **Include a folder** *button and navigate to the folder that you want to include. (You may navigate anywhere on your system where you have access, including locations shared through HomeGroup.)*

3 *Highlight the name of the folder that you want to include – in this
case the folder House – and click on the* **Include folder** *button.*

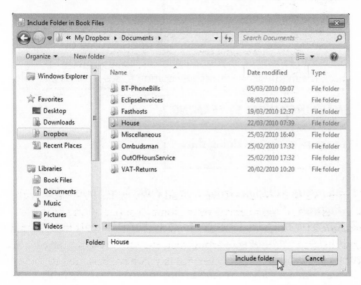

Windows will now list the folders and files that you have added
and you can access them in the usual way.

If you delete the top level library icon – in this example Book
Files – by choosing Delete from the context menu you will
remove it from the library but the files that it contains will
remain intact in their original locations. If you delete a file or
folder from inside the library – such as the House folder in
this example – its contents will be deleted from their original
location. You have been warned!

Streaming media

Whenever you access music or video (such as a Youtube clip) from
the Internet you are streaming media to your system. Windows 7
takes the principle a bit further by giving you the tools to send

media streams across your HomeGroup network to other PCs running Windows 7.

> You may also be able to stream media to dedicated hardware equipment – stereo/TV/etc. – though this is beyond the scope of this book. However, if your equipment has an Ethernet port, check the manufacturer's documentation to see if this is possible.

ENABLING MEDIA STREAMING

There are two ways of doing this.

Either:
1 *Navigate to HomeGroup and tick the box 'Stream My Pictures....'*
2 *Click on the* **Save Changes** *button (note the warning that media streaming is not secure).*

Or:
1 *Start Media Player by clicking on the icon near the* **Start** *button.*
2 *If it is in Player mode – see figure – click on the button to change to Library mode.*

3 *Select the* **Stream** *button from the top menu bar, then click on Turn on Home Media Streaming. Note that if this option isn't available from the* **Stream** *menu, this means that streaming is already enabled.*
Whichever method you choose your media streams will be available to all members of your HomeGroup unless you decide to modify this.

CONTROLLING ACCESS TO MEDIA STREAMS

In order to fine-tune who can see what:

1 *Click on the* **Stream** *button in Media Player.*

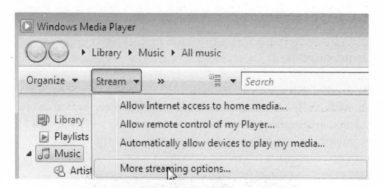

2 *Click on More streaming options. You will now see the default settings for streaming to devices in your HomeGroup. The following figure shows a network of two computers.*

By default, everyone has access to everything. As you can see from the figure there are options to block everything or to block individual devices. For each device there is also a customize option which allows you to filter content along much the same lines as you would Parental Controls.

Choose media streaming options for computers and devices

Name your media library: Anthony
Choose default settings...

Show devices on: Local network ▾

Allow All   Block All

Media programs on this PC and remote connections...
Allowed access using default settings.
Allowed ▾

STEINBECK   Customize...   Allowed ▾
Allowed access using default settings.   Remove...

All devices are allowed to access your shared media.

Choose homegroup and sharing options
Choose power options
Tell me more about media streaming
Read the privacy statement online

Cloud storage

These are third-party services which allow you to save files to a remote server on the Internet and synchronize them across several systems. Because these services are nothing to do with Windows – or, indeed, Microsoft – you can share and synchronize files across all supported operating systems.

The two main players in this form of storage are DropBox and UbuntuOne. Both offer remote storage of a couple of gigabytes free in the hope that users will like the system and buy more storage for a monthly fee.

DropBox supports: Windows – all versions, MacOS X, Linux and iPhone

UbuntuOne only supports Linux at present (April 2010) but a Windows version is under development.

INSTALLING DROPBOX

1 *Go to the DropBox site and download the installer by clicking on the* **Download** *button.*

2 *Click on the downloaded installer and follow the on-screen instructions. If this is a new account you will need to fill in an on-line form and provide a valid e-mail address (which will be your user ID) and a password.*

3 *Choose your account type (2 Gb Free is good for starters) and click on* **Next**.

4 *Accept the default values suggested by the installer until you reach the final screen.*
5 *Click on the* **Finish** *button.*

You now have a new My DropBox folder as a sub-folder of your My Documents folder, like this:

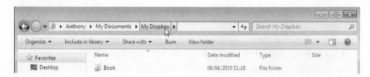

Now that you have a DropBox folder any files that you put in it will be backed up to the remote server that holds your account on the DropBox site and all changes are synchronized when they are made. If, for example, you accidentally delete a file you can go to the DropBox site and recover it. For free accounts this can be done any time within 30 days.

ADDING A SECOND PC

If you install a copy of DropBox on a second computer you can synchronize your files across both systems, i.e. with the remote file store and with each other. Because it is cross-platform you can synchronize files between (say) an Apple Mac notebook and a Windows PC, or a Linux PC and netbook or tablet. As with so many things, the best way to explore this is to have a go at it.

THINGS TO REMEMBER

1 *HomeGroup only works for a Home network as defined by Windows 7. If you are having problems, check your settings in Control Panel.*

2 *If you have lost or forgotten the HomeGroup password go to the PC that you used to set up the HomeGroup, navigate to HomeGroup settings and click on the View or Print the HomeGroup Password link.*

3 *Be sure that you are using the correct type of Ethernet cable. Use a straight-through cable to connect to a switch/router; use a crossover to connect two PCs back-to-back.*

4 *If you delete a Library the files that it contains are unaffected. If you delete files or folders from inside a Library they will be deleted from the original locations.*

5 *You can control access to Media streams through Windows Media Player.*

6 *Cloud storage – such as DropBox – allows you to share and synchronize files across different locations and operating systems.*

18

Wireless networking

In this chapter you will learn:
- *how to set up an ad hoc wireless connection*
- *how to set up a wireless access point*
- *how to secure you wireless network*

Wireless networking has become increasingly popular with home users in recent years. It offers a lot of flexibility, particularly if you take a laptop/notebook computer between home and office.

Anything that you can do with a wired network can also be done wirelessly and with a few simple precautions, a wireless network can be as secure as its wired counterpart.

Wireless Networking Standards

There are several wireless networking standards, but only two of these are likely to be of interest to the home user. These are the 802.11g and 802.11n standards.

There is also an older 802.11b standard but this is legacy kit and should be avoided if possible.

The current standard – 11n – is faster than 11g and is also backward compatible with earlier standards. Whatever you decide to buy, check your existing equipment and make sure that your new kit is backward compatible with it as some users report that there are still some compatibility issues.

INSTALLING A WIRELESS ADAPTER

Laptop and notebook systems almost invariably have wireless connectivity built in to them. Desktop systems will probably need to be fitted with a wireless network adapter. The choice is between a PCI/PCI-e card fitted in an expansion slot on the motherboard or a USB adapter. Whichever option you choose, the installation proceeds along the same lines. Obviously you should read all manufacturer's documentation that came with the product and make sure that you have the appropriate drivers on disk – either a download or a CD distributed with the product. Unless the documentation advises you otherwise, the installation process goes like this:

1 *Install the drivers from the manufacturer's disk.*
2 *Attach the adapter. You will need to power down the system and observe anti-static precautions for an internal card or simply plug the card into the USB port for a USB adapter.*
3 *With the adapter in place, configure the connection in Windows.*
4 *Connect to the wireless network.*

A WORKED EXAMPLE

This example walks through the installation of a Belkin wireless-N USB adapter on a desktop system running Windows 7 Home Premium.

1 *Put the driver CD into the CDROM drive. If it doesn't autoplay, then navigate to the setup file on the disk and click on it to start the installation process. Skip over the warning from Windows about the unsigned driver to run the installer. You will be prompted to provide a location for the drivers. Accept the suggested default folder and click on* **Next** *to continue.*

2 *When prompted to do so, put the USB adapter in the USB port.*

3 *You will then be prompted to reboot your system. Click on the* **Finish** *button to do this.*

4 *After the reboot, click on the System Tray connection icon to see your new connection.*

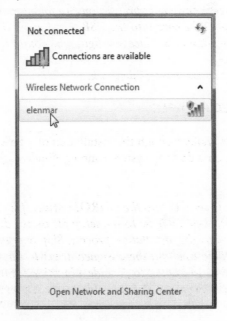

5 *Click on the name of the network that you want to connect to, and note the tick box option to make this an automatic action. If you select this you will connect to this network by default just as you would to your wired home network.*

Ad-hoc wireless networks

The simplest type of wireless network is known as an ad-hoc network because it has no formal structure. It may consist of a couple of wireless-enabled PCs which network when they are in range of one another. This is the easiest way of communicating between a laptop/notebook system – most of which are wireless-enabled out of the box – and a desktop machine that has a wireless network connection on board, or installed via an expansion slot on the motherboard.

TO SET UP YOUR AD-HOC WIRELESS NETWORK:

1 *Navigate to Network and Sharing Center (through the Control Panel) and click on the link to Set Up a New Connection or Network.*
2 *Scroll to the bottom of the options list, select the Setup a Wireless Ad Hoc... option and click on the **Next** button.*
3 *Read the notes on ad-hoc networks that Windows presents, then click on **Next**.*
4 *Choose a name and security password for your new network. Note the tick box options to conceal the password – generally a good idea – and the option to make this a permanent connection. Click on **Next** to proceed.*

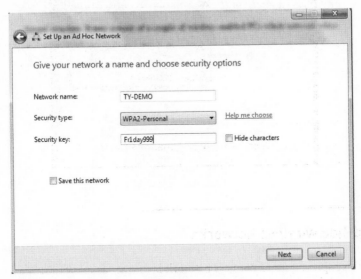

5 *Windows will now confirm your new setup and give you the opportunity to turn on Internet Connection Sharing.*

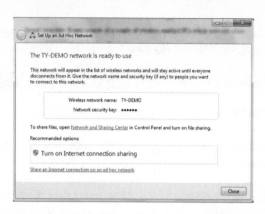

6 *Choose your options and click on the* **Close** *button to finish.*

TO ACCESS YOUR AD-HOC WIRELESS NETWORK:

1 *Go to another wireless enabled PC on your network and click on the connect icon in the System Tray. You will see something like this – a click on the new network entry in the list.*

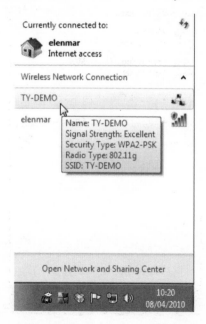

2 *Click on* **Connect.** *You will now be prompted for the security key (password). Enter the key.*

3 *Click on* **OK** *to connect.*
4 *Click on the Connection icon in the System Tray again to see the status of your new connection.*

Note from this figure that Internet Connection Sharing is not available. This is because we didn't enable it at step 5 of the setup process.

Using an ad-hoc connection

By default an ad-hoc connection is a temporary arrangement which will expire when the PC where it was set up is turned off. See step 4 of the setup process above. You can, however, make this a permanent arrangement by ticking the appropriate box during setup. A possible application for this would be to have your main PC set up for Internet access and make this permanently available for your laptop whenever it comes within range (about 30 feet). In this case you are, in effect, using the 'main' PC as a wireless access point and its shared Internet connection as a router.

Wireless access points

A Wireless Access Point (WAP) – sometimes known as a Base Station – is the wireless equivalent of a hub or switch on a wired network. It can be attached to a conventional wired network to provide a connection for wireless enabled systems. Although it is beyond the scope of this book, which deals only with PCs running Windows, a Wireless Access Point will enable you to connect any computer, such as a Mac or a PC running a different operating system, so long as it supports wireless networking and the encryption type you have chosen.

For most home users these days, WAP functionality is built into an ADSL modem/router which also provides wireless access and an Ethernet switch all in the same hardware unit. However, the principles and techniques needed to implement them are the same regardless of the physical packaging.

SETTING UP YOUR WAP

The procedures for setting up your Wireless Access Point are broadly similar to setting up an Internet connection through a router – see *Connecting your router* in Chapter 15. Your WAP will have at least one – probably more – Ethernet ports for connection to a wired LAN. Obviously you will need to read and follow any installation instructions from the manufacturer, but the general procedure is to attach a PC to the LAN port of the WAP and do any necessary configuration tasks.

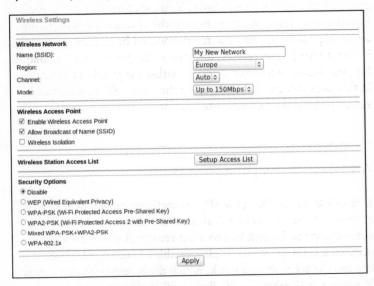

This figure shows the WAP setup page on a Netgear ADSL modem/router. Most of the fields are sensible defaults and should be left as they are unless you have good reason to change them.

The four key fields for our present purposes are the name (SSID) of the network, the boxes to enable wireless access and to broadcast the SSID to anyone coming into range, and Security which is currently disabled. This last is obviously something of a security hole and we shall return to it later in the chapter. For the time being, make your selections and click on **Apply**.

CONNECTING TO YOUR WAP

1 *Click on the connection icon in the System Tray. You will see something like this:*

2 *Click on the My New Network entry in the list. You will see something like this. Note from the figure that this is an insecure network and that you have the option to make this an automatic connection.*

3 *Click on* **Connect.**

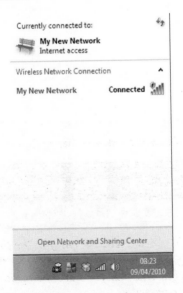

You are now connected to your new wireless network.

Wireless security

TURNING OFF SSID BROADCASTING

The simplest form of security is to turn off the SSID broadcast from your WAP. This means that Windows will still detect the existence of your network and will list it on the menu from the connection icon in the System Tray as Other Network.

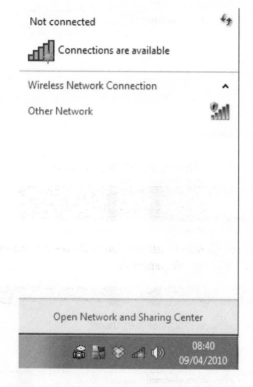

1 *Click on Other Network and you will be prompted to connect in the usual way.*

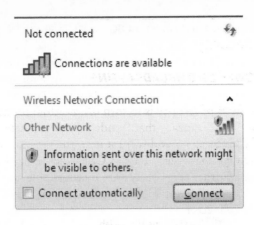

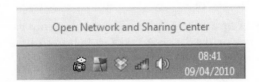

2 *Click on the* **Connect** *button. You will now be prompted to enter the SSID for the network.*

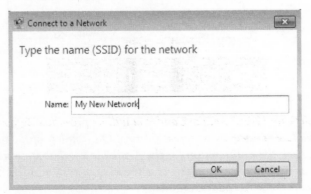

3 *Enter the SSID and click on* **OK**.

Note that the SSID is case-sensitive – *M*Y *New Network* is NOT
the same as *My New Network* – so by choosing something
memorable but not too predictable like (say) Friday-996 you have,
in effect, password-protected your new connection.

ACCESS LISTS

You can add a further layer of security by restricting access to
particular PCs based on the Media Access Control (MAC) address
of their LAN connectors.

> Every network adapter has a unique 'burnt on' hardware
> address in the form of six hexadecimal fields that looks like:
> 00-30-BD-F9-47-32. If you want to see the MAC address of
> your network adapter, open a command prompt and type
> 'getmac' [Enter].

In order to set up an access list navigate to the setup page of your
WAP and click on the **Set up Access List** button (see the figure
above) this will take you to a page that looks like this:

1 *Tick the box to turn Access Control On (top left of the figure).*
2 *Check the radio button for the Available wireless station that
has been detected – in this case the known system ASIMOV
with the MAC address shown.*

3 *Click on* **ADD.**

Wireless Station Access List		
☑ **Turn Access Control On**		
Trusted Wireless Stations		
	Device Name	MAC Address
⊙	ASIMOV	00:30:BD:F9:47:C2
	Delete	
Available Wireless Stations		
	Device Name	MAC Address
	Add	

As you can see from the figure the system ASIMOV has been added to the Trusted Wireless Stations list.

4 *Click on* **Apply** *to make your changes permanent.*

You can repeat steps 2–4 for every system that you wish to add, and only these trusted systems will be able access your network.

> If you change the physical network adapter in any of your PCs it will of course have a different MAC address and will need to be added to the Access Control List as a new system.

For most home users the security measures outlined so far are probably adequate; all you want is to prevent casual use by neighbours or anyone else who comes into range.

Other security measures

If you navigate to the setup screen of your WAP you will see the security options that are available.

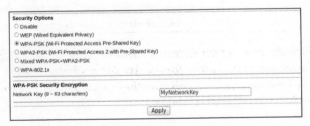

Security Options
○ Disable
○ WEP (Wired Equivalent Privacy)
⊙ WPA-PSK (Wi-Fi Protected Access Pre-Shared Key)
○ WPA2-PSK (Wi-Fi Protected Access 2 with Pre-Shared Key)
○ Mixed WPA-PSK+WPA2-PSK
○ WPA-802.1x
WPA-PSK Security Encryption
Network Key (8 – 63 characters)   MyNetworkKey
Apply

All of these – apart from None – are means of setting a password that is encrypted so that it cannot be intercepted when sent over the wireless link. We will step through one of them as an example.

1 *Choose your security preference.*
2 *Enter a key – preferably something easy to remember but hard to guess.*
3 *Save your choices by clicking on* **Apply***.*
4 *Go to one of the wireless enabled systems and click on the connection icon. You will be presented with a prompt like this:*

5 *Enter the Security Key in order to connect.*

Using SSID as a password (see Turning off SSID Broadcasting, above) involves sending an unencrypted password over your wireless network. The other methods use varying types and strengths of encryption. It is possible, with the right equipment, to intercept wireless signals so encryption adds a layer of security. For most home users the probability of anyone cracking their system – as opposed to merely finding an open, unprotected network – is fairly low.

THINGS TO REMEMBER

1 Wireless networks offer the same range of facilities as wired networks – file sharing, printer sharing, etc. – but without the wires.

2 Wireless connections are not as secure 'out of the box' as their wired equivalents but they can be secured with a few simple steps.

3 The latest versions of the wireless standards are designed to be backward compatible with earlier equipment but it still pays the check before you buy.

4 Laptop and Notebook systems are wireless-enabled as a matter of course. You may need to add a network adapter – internal or USB – to connect a desktop system wirelessly.

5 The least you should do for security is to turn off SSID broadcast.

6 Whatever security you implement use strong passwords. Password and drowssap have been done before. Choose something that contains non-alphabetic characters or use a language other than your own. For example 'Friday' is weak, 'Friday-999' is better, and 'Vrijdag-23' is better still, though all of them are based on the name of the day of the week.

Index

Abiword word processor, *168*
    installing, *168*
    setting up, *170*
Action Center, *39*
Administrator rights, *3*
anti-virus software, *243*
anti-virus software, scheduling, *247*
applications
    installing, *168*
    reinstalling, *202*
    removing, *163*
Autoplay, *51*
AVG software, installing, *244*

backup media, *80*
    rotating sets, *85*
backup tools, 14, *16*
backups, *79*
    differential, *84*
    disk cloning, *83*
    disk imaging, *83*
    full, *84*
    incremental, *84*
    network, *82*
    restoring from, *18*
batch files, *75*
boot options, *10*
boot sector virus, *253*
broadband Internet connection, *227*
broadband modem/router
    connecting, *231*
    installing, *230*

CD/DVD disks, writable, *80*
CD/DVD drives, *96*
Check Disk, *3, 215*
cleaning products, *126*
cloud storage, *272*
CMD scripts, *75*
CMOS battery, *98*
CMOS/BIOS settings, *86*
    accessing, *87*
    checking, *189*
command line prompt, *67*
    accessing, *68*

    common commands, *71*
    exercise, *70*
    help, *74*
    syntax, *69*
components, replacing, *xvi*
connections, cleaning, *129*
Control Panel, *34–54*
    search utiliy, *36*
    views, *34*
CPU, *93*

Date and Time, *37–8*
default programs, *173*
    setting, *177*
Defender, *249*
defragging, *6*
device drivers
    installing, *143*
    signed, *144*
    updating, *208*
Device Manager, *41, 206*
devices
    adding, *50*
    troubleshooting, *206*
dialup connections, *223*
directories, and folders, *68*
Disk Cleanup Wizard, *4, 29*
disk cloning, *83*
Disk Defragmenter, *6*
disk drives
    adding, *108*
    controllers, *94*
    jumper settings, *109*
    master and slave, *109*
    partitioning, *110*
    removable, *82*
disk imaging, *83*
Display settings, *47*
documentation, finding online, *xx*
DOS prompt, *67*
Dropbox, *273*

Ease of Access Center, *48*
Easy Transfer wizard, *184*
    restoring with, *199*

e-mail, types, *239*
Ethernet, *258*

family safety, *44*
file types and programs, *174*
files, clearing temporary, *4*
firewalsl, *40, 236*
Firewire, *142*
floppy disk drives, *97*
    adding, *115*
Folder Options, *49*
Fonts, *49*

gadgets, *47*
graphics cards, *97*

hardware
    diagnosing problems,
     210
    working with, *90*
Hardware and Sound settings, *50*
Help Desk, *56*
    calling, *62*
HomeGroup, *xvii, 259*
    creating, *261*
    viewing, *263*

information, gathering, *58*
ink jet printers, *148*
InPrivate browsing, *252*
Internet, *xx*
    dialup connection, *223*
    settings, *222*
Internet connection, *221*
    troubleshooting, *234*
Internet Explorer
    InPrivate browsing, *252*
    protection, *249*

jumper settings, *109*

laser printers, *149*
libraries, *267*
    adding files, *268*
    creating, *267*
Live Mail, settings, *183*

mail server information, *60*
maintenance, *124*
    cleaning, *126*
    schedule, *124*

malware, *242*
modem
    installing, *223*
    USB broadband, *227*
Molex connectors, *95*
monitors
    cleaning, *127*
    installing, *137*
motherboard, *92*
    replacing, *120*
Mouse options, *51*
MSCONFIG, *216*

network addresses, *230*
Network Discovery, *xvii*
networking, *257*
    connections, *258*
    HomeGroup, *259*
    wireless, *277*
networks
    and printers, *156, 264*

OEM install, *188*
old equipment, disposal of,
   131
optical drives, *96*
    replacing, *114*

parallel ports, *138*
    and printers, *152*
Parental Controls, *44*
    Internet, *252*
passwords, *59*
PC technicians, *62*
    qualifications, *65*
PCI expansion cards, *98*
    fitting, *118*
PCI-e cards, *98*
    fitting, *119*
performance options, *8*
peripheral devices, *134*
Personalization options, *47*
phishing, *250*
plug and play, *50*
    printers, *153*
POP3, e-mail service, *239*
ports, *134*
    keyboard and mouse, *135*
    modem, *136*
    network, *136*
    parallel, *138*

ports *(Contd)*
    serial, *139*
    USB, *139*
Power Options, *43*
power supply unit (PSU), *95*
    replacing, *106*
printers, *147*
    connecting, *152*
    installing, *154*
    multi-function, *151*
    online support, *158*
    sharing over network, *156, 264*
    troubleshooting, *160*
    types, *148*
problems, defining, *57*
programs, searching for, *6*

RAM, *94*
    adding, *103*
Region and Language options, *53*
removable disk drives, *82*
    cleaning, *130*
repair disk, *15*
    and viruses, *253*
Repair your Computer, *11*
restore points, *27*
    removing, *28*

Safe Mode, *9*
safety issues, hardware, *131*
Search, *6*
Serial ATA (SATA) drives, *95*
serial ports, *139*
shadow copies, *31*
SmartScreen Filter, *250*
SMTP, e-mail service, *239*
Sound options, *52*
SSID, security, *288*
SSID, *285*
Startup Repair, *12*
streaming media, *270*
support calls, *56*
surge suppressors, *131*
System and Security settings, *39*
system box, inside, *91*
system image, *19*
    restoring, *21–24*
System information, *xxi, 41, 214*
System Recovery, *11*
System Restore, *12, 24–27*

tape drives, *81*
    adding, *115*
Task Manager, *166*
Taskbar and Start menu options, *48*
trojans, *242*
troubleshooting, *204*
    common problems, *218*
    reproducing problems, *213*

uninstalling applications, *163*
upgrading hardware, *102*
    when not to, *99*
USB
    broadband modem, *227*
    connectors, *141*
    ports, *139*
    printer connection, *153*
    speeds, *140*
user accounts, *44*

viruses, *242*
    anti-virus software, *243*
    AVG software, *244*
    boot sector, *253*
    dealing with, *253*
visual effects, *8*

Windows 7
    editions, *1*
    installing, *190*
    reinstalling, *179*
Windows components, *173*
Windows Defender, *249*
Windows Firewall, *40, 237*
Windows Live Mail, settings, *183*
Windows Memory Diagnostic,
12, 216
Windows Update, *42*
Windows versions, *1*
    checking, *xiv*
    compatibility, *xv*
Windows Vista, *2*
Windows XP, *2*
wireless access points (WAP), *284*
    setting up, *285*
wireless networking, *277*
    ad-hoc, *280*
    installing, *278*
    security, *291*
worms, *242*